Dancing at the Devil's Party

POETS ON POETRY

David Lehman, General Editor
Donald Hall, Founding Editor

Alicia Suskin Ostriker

Dancing at the Devil's Party

ESSAYS ON POETRY,
POLITICS, AND
THE EROTIC

Ann Arbor

THE UNIVERSITY OF MICHIGAN PRESS

Copyright © by the University of Michigan 2000
All rights reserved
Published in the United States of America by
The University of Michigan Press
Manufactured in the United States of America
∞ Printed on acid-free paper

2003   2002   2001   2000   4   3   2   1

A CIP catalog record for this book is available from the British Library.

Library of Congress Cataloging-in-Publication Data

Ostriker, Alicia.
    Dancing at the devil's party : essays on poetry, politics, and the
    erotic / Alicia Suskin Ostriker.
        p. cm. — (Poets on poetry)
    Includes bibliographical references.
    ISBN 0-472-09696-6 (alk. paper)—ISBN 0-472-06696-X (pbk. :
    alk. paper)
    1. American poetry—History and criticism.   I. Title. II. Series.
PS305.075   2000
811.009—dc21
                                                    99-047945

for J. P. O.
with gratitude

Contents

Preface

"Poetry makes nothing happen," said W. H. Auden, but there are those of us who disagree. Poetry can tear at the heart with its claws, make the neural nets shiver, flood us with hope, despair, longing, ecstasy, love, anger, terror. It can help us think more lucidly. It can force us to laugh. Poetry can, as Conrad puts it, make us *see*. It can also, like Rilke's torso of Apollo, tell us that we must change our lives. From time to time, some of us believe, poetry changes the world. I am of this (perhaps dotty) persuasion and I have always enjoyed the work of visionary artists dissatisfied with the rule of "things as they are." In the present selection of essays composed during the years following the 1986 publication of my book on American women's poetry, *Stealing the Language*, I continue to fish in the stream of my obsession.

I find myself still drawn, of course, to women's poetry, especially where it runs against the current of what is respectably well mannered. Questions about poetic form and style, and how prosodic structures alchemize into meaning, intrigue me, along with questions about the myriad ways poems can grapple with political and social issues without collapsing into propaganda. An essay is my way of pursuing an elusive intuition into the forest of what I cannot yet understand. What does the women's poetry movement mean in aesthetic terms? How many different kinds of love can I locate in Whitman, and what happens when I run up against his Civil War poetry? Why am I irritated when a critic sets up an opposition between Elizabeth Bishop and Sharon Olds? What makes Maxine Kumin's nature poetry different from other nature poetry? What makes the apparent simplicity of Lucille Clifton so resonant, and how do

I, as white reader, respond to a black writer? What is Jewish about Allen Ginsberg's "Howl"?

As my own poetry has come increasingly to wrestle with issues of spirituality in general and what Judaism signifies to me in particular, I have become fascinated by convergences of the political, the erotic, and the spiritual in other poets. Although none of the poets discussed in this book walk exactly the path I do, they feel proximate. Shelley said that we are all engaged in the writing of a collective poem, and there is a sense in which all the poets I have chosen to explore here—varied though their surfaces appear—belong to the devil's party of those who pursue desire rather than bow to reason. In a postmodern era there is something embarrassing about this, and I feel acutely how unfashionable my taste for a poetics of ardor is. So much the more am I obliged to champion it, to offer the shawl of my words against the chill. "All that I have is a voice," as Auden says in another poem, "to undo the folded lie." What lie? Reader, that is for you to discern.

Dancing at the Devil's Party

Some Notes on Politics and Poetry

> If you/I hesitate to speak, isn't it because we are afraid of
> not speaking well? But what is "well" or "badly?" With
> what are we conforming if we speak "well?" What
> hierarchy, what subordination lurks there, waiting to break
> our resistance? What claim to raise ourselves up in a
> worthier discourse? Erection is no business of ours: we are
> at home in the flatlands.
> —Luce Irigaray, "When Our Lips Speak Together"

I. The Devil's Party

My education in political poetry begins with William Blake's
remark about John Milton in *The Marriage of Heaven and Hell:*
"The reason Milton wrote in fetters when he wrote of Angels
& God, and at liberty when of Devils & Hell, is because he was
a true Poet and of the Devil's party without knowing it." The
statement is usually taken as a charming misreading of Milton
or as some sort of hyperbole. We find it lumped with other
readings that supposedly view Satan as the hero of *Paradise
Lost,* such as Percy Bysshe Shelley's in *A Defence of Poetry,* al-
though neither Blake nor Shelley says anything of the kind.

I consider Blake's statement simply accurate. I think it the
best single thing anybody has ever said about *Paradise Lost.* If
not clear as a bell, then at least as compressed as diamonds. The
insouciant opening gesture takes for granted what to Blake
(and to me) is obvious: that the poetry qua poetry is better,

more exciting, more energetic, in the sections dominated by Satan, and worse, duller, less poetic, in the sections dominated by God. As a lover of poetry, Blake has evidently struck a perplexity. Why (he asks himself) does Milton's Satan excite me and his God bore me even though he plainly intends me to adore God and scorn Satan? The answer could have been that Milton "wrote in fetters" where constrained by theology and the danger of lapsing into inadvertant sacrilege, but "at liberty" otherwise. Other critics have claimed that it is impossible to make God talk successfully in a poem, but the Book of Job is enough to refute that position. Why did Milton choose to make God talk at all? Dante cleverly avoided that difficulty.

The second half of Blake's sentence not only solves the *Paradise Lost* problem but proposes a radical view of all poetry, which might be summarized as follows: All art depends on opposition between God and the devil, reason and energy. The true poet (the good poet) is necessarily the partisan of energy, rebellion, and desire, and is opposed to passivity, obedience, and the authority of reason, laws, and institutions. To be a poet requires energy; energetic subjects make the best material for poems; the truer (better) the poetry, the more it will embody the truths of Desire. But the poet need not think so. He can be of the devil's party without knowing it.

The metaphoric train of Blake's sentence is as significant as its idea. "No ideas but in metaphors" might be a useful rule of thumb for poets and critics, especially when we engage in ideological discourse, where words so easily collapse into formulaic wallpaper. A metaphor gives us at least a fighting chance of saying something real. "Fetters . . . liberty . . . party" announces that the theological issue in *Paradise Lost* is inseparable from the political issue. "Are not Religion and Politics the Same Thing?" Blake asks elsewhere. "Prisons are built with stones of Law, Brothels with bricks of Religion," one of the pungently metaphorical Proverbs of Hell, draws the parallels neatly: in each case an authoritarian system must create something to punish. Law begets Crime, Religion begets Sin. A century and a half later Michel Foucault reinvents this particular wheel.

But to return to *Paradise Lost:* As William Empson long ago observed, Milton's God (which is really to say Christianity's God, in the moment of Milton's writing) is a model tyrant. He is also disagreeably egocentric, legalistic, self-justifying, and dull. Milton's Satan on the other hand is not at all a good fellow, but he is fascinating and complex—passionate, intelligent, eloquent, capable of introspection, responsive to experience and situation, sexually attractive (as in the scene where Eve is fascinated by the sinuous form of the serpent), and arousable. He can be haughty, humiliated, despairing, hopeful, awed, jealous, spiteful, self-deluding, generous, resolute, exhausted. He is one of us. He is interesting. Milton's God is at best a schoolmaster, at worst Blake's nasty Noboddaddy. And all this is conveyed quite magnificently by Milton's own poetry. At the same time, Milton unquestionably intended to justify God's ways to men, as a poet "enchanted" (C. S. Lewis's splendid term in the *Preface to Paradise Lost*) by the idea of Hierarchy and the beauty of Obedience.

Milton's God-Satan opposition illustrates the way repression inevitably precipitates rebellion. His Adam and Eve demonstrate a parallel inevitability attending gender stratification. "He for God only, she for God in him." Adam is supposed to (benignly) lead and guide, as he has been created with the fuller measure of Reason. Eve is supposed to (voluntarily) follow, having been created with enough Reason to appreciate how wise and superior Adam is, but not enough to be independently trustworthy, due to her overdose of Passion. What Milton's God has wrought, in other words, is an intrinsically unstable system. It has to break down, and it does break down as soon as Eve realizes that she does not like being the dominated and "inferior" half of the couple. Hierarchy, in the instant that it crosses the line from description to prescription, invites defiance. From the moment we meet Adam and Eve we see the crack in the crockery. It is going to break, it is going to—ah, it has broken. Naturally Eve is more interesting poetically than Adam, who is a well-meaning fellow but a bit of a stiff.

If the true poet is of the devil's party without knowing it, what happens when the poet sets forth with malice aforethought as a devil's advocate? Well, Byron's self-conscious satanic heroes are almost as boring as Milton's God. De Sade, that self-conscious satanist, is not boring only because he is of God's party without knowing it, the hysterical Sadean railings against priests, nuns, virtue, motherhood, and so on, indicating the presence of a particularly virulent superego that he persisted in trying to crush. Blake himself, radical as he was, harbored an unacknowledged seed of orthodoxy in the longing for certitude and transcendence that ultimately sprouted and flourished in his late prophecies. Like Milton, Blake contains within himself both sides of a monumental and age-old political, cultural, and psychic quarrel, played out on the fields of religion and myth.

But beyond good and evil? Beyond dominance and obedience? Beyond the dualities, however excitingly charged and contradictory? Of course: plurality. The world remains a continuum, infinite in all directions, and the artist defies (our, his, her) impulse to interpret everything dualistically, first by containing both halves of any argument and then by the attempt to imitate the continuum. All trades: their gear and tackle and trim. The Whitman catalogue, which delights by its scurry and randomness as we are delighted by the spectacle of a city street. The hundred unique characters of Shakespeare, trooping in their rings of alliance and conflict, each doubtless representing a vitally debatable political position, but in bulk representing an infinite variety that ultimately dwarfs debate. From *The Merchant of Venice* we can argue pro and con anti-Semitism, from *Lear* pro and con patriarchal absolutism, from *Antony and Cleopatra* the claims of the state against those of eros—but *The Complete Plays of Shakespeare* argues the smallness of argument.

Or think of the Chaucer of whom Dryden exclaimed: Here is God's plenty. The man who imagined the Wife of Bath, with her gat-tooth, her debater's points against clerical misogyny, and her six or seven husbands, is the first feminist poet in English. And when we recall that he imagined as well the pious and priggish Prioress, the high-minded Knight, the low-minded Miller, the slimy Pardoner, the inocent Troilus, the experienced Cressida, and so forth, it is astonishing that scholars have tried to reduce Chaucer to a Christian or a courtier: to confine him to an ideology. I believe, though I cannot prove, that the plenteousness of great writers is always their most radical quality, in that it implicitly defies category and authority. Exuberance, says Blake, is beauty. In whatever age, and whatever the writer's ostensible political positions, plenitude and exuberance signal the democratizing/subversive impulse, the dance of the devil's party.

In *A Defence of Poetry* Shelley says, "The great secret of morals is love; or a going out of our own nature. . . . A man, to be greatly good, must imagine intensely and comprehensively; he must put himself in the place of another and of many others." I take this to mean that we first crack the wall between ourselves and our enemy, discovering the foe within the self. Then we find that we and the world are neither single nor double but multiple.

II. Loving (and) Contradiction

"Trust thyself: every heart vibrates to that iron string." So urges Emerson. As the creation of the poem depends on this, so does the reading of it. I mean actual reading; what we do ourselves, for pleasure.

Suspicious as I am of theory, which is always prescribing to me what I should prefer and interfering with my personal responses, I want to stress the importance of a lively response to the political as to any other aspect of a poem. If a work fails to arouse me, how can I begin to understand it, much less judge it?

Yet there are different kinds of arousals. First of all, and let us be candid about this, we love what is on our side. Poems by Blake, Whitman, William Carlos Williams, Allen Ginsberg, for example, in my own case. The critic who attempts to disguise advocacy, pretending to possess aesthetic standards without ideological implications, is not to be trusted—nor did any critic of major stature pretend to do so until the late nineteenth century. Yet we can also become excited in the presence of the enemy camp, if someone whose work runs contrary to our deep convictions is writing strongly enough to crystallize our differences. Eliot, for example, in my own case. Mild and waspish, lost without the crutch of authority and orthodoxy, snob, anti-Semite, gynephobe—how beautifully he shows me the beauty of what I must struggle to oppose. Or, a more obvious and violent sort of foe, the LeRoi Jones of "Black Art" advocating "poems that kill" in the sleekest of jive rhythms, proving the attractiveness of hate. I like to think that I love in political poetry whatever I love in poetry anyway. Language known and used by someone who delights in the lay of words together. Wit, grace, passion, eloquence, playfulness, compression, vitality, freshness. A voice that is at once the poet's voice and the voice of a time, a nation, a gender. The many, mysteriously funneled through the one: not I, not I, but the wind that blows through me. Only I hope to be aware that "whatever I love in poetry anyway" has, if I cut into it, a political dimension.

I prefer the word "love" to the word "evaluate." Bring out number, weight, and measure in a year of dearth, says Blake. I find "love" more reliable than "evaluate." First I see what I love, then I try to understand it. In this way it seems I can love one thing and another, each for different reasons, rather than the same thing over and over and smaller and smaller.

Take Elizabeth Bishop's "Brazil, January 1, 1502," with its brilliant description of a tropic landscape as if it were a tapestry or an embroidery, followed by a description of "the Christians, hard as nails, / tiny as nails, and glinting, / in a creaking armor," who arrive with a dream of "wealth . . . plus a brand-new pleasure":

> Directly after Mass, humming perhaps
> L'Homme armé or some such tune,
> they ripped away into the hanging fabric,
> each out to catch an Indian for himself—
> those maddening little women who kept calling,
> calling to each other (or had the birds waked up?)
> and retreating, always retreating, behind it.[1]

The women are like the female lizard Bishop has earlier pictured, "her wicked tail straight up and over, / red as a red-hot wire." The poem delicately and ironically manipulates the parallel between women and land, alike subject to ripping/raping. In its resemblance to a just-finished embroidery, the landscape has already been feminized; the goddess who by implication has stitched it would naturally madden "the Christians." At the same time, the mediation of this embroidery conceit along with Bishop's casual half-amused tone, which throughout the poem negotiates slyly between the perspective of a twentieth-century viewer and that of a sixteenth-century conquistador, frames and distances our horror at the brutality to which the poem alludes. Finally, Bishop's conclusion implies, though in an equally bemused way, that the landscape and its natives may have been, may remain, mysteriously unconquerable.

Given the historical realities of conquest, rape, the slave trade, and genocide in Brazil and elsewhere, this conclusion is itself a bit maddening to me. I instinctively look for more bitterness, more denunciation, some recognition that although Nature may be unconquerable, individual lives and cultures are not. Witholding these gratifications to my (perhaps correct) opinions, Bishop instead reminds me that a conqueror's rapacity may be insatiable precisely because it can never feel that it has truly possessed what it has conquered. This is a still more distressing thought and a sharp insight into the mentality of colonialism. As a consequence of Bishop's artistry, whenever I reread "Brazil, January 1, 1502," I am seduced anew by its fascinatingly elusive mix of calm and anger, disturbed anew by the sense of how rooted in the erotic and the sacred is the will toward empire.

Here is a part of another poem on the theme of conquest, using the same idea that the conquerors justify their acts by perceiving the conquered as animals. Untitled, it is by Lydia Yellowbird:

> When you came
>   you found a people
>   with red skin
>   they were one
>   with all living things
>
> But you did not see this
>   beauty
>   instead you saw them
>   as animals, primitive
>   savage.[2]

Next to Bishop's poem Yellowbird's is embarrassingly naive. It lacks irony and distance, its language is banal and abstract, it fails to imagine (as against stating) what the enemy "saw," and so it has no poetic interests beyond its message. Any poetry that is merely political—and nothing else—is shallow poetry, although it may serve a valuable temporary purpose. This is the difference between poetry and propaganda. Yet if I heard Yellowbird's piece performed, let's say, in Santa Fe to the right audience, in all its shrill shallowness, I might well be more stirred by it than by the Bishop poem. Do I contradict myself? Very well then, I contradict myself. Another example: after a Ginsberg reading at Rutgers, I asked a graduate student of radical bent how she liked him. Well, he had been singing Blake's "Tiger," and she had been sitting there in the front row under his knees while he bounced his harmonium up and down and wagged his body around, for what seemed like forever. It was embarrassing. And had she not read Bakhtin, I asked, and did she not notice that Ginsberg's performance was *carnivalesque*? Oh, that's right, she said; it's so different when it's real life.

III.   Changing the Music

The poetry I know best, just now, is contemporary American women's poetry. When I began reading this body of work in the mid-1970s, it was speaking to me as woman and as poet in ways no other poetry ever had. Repeatedly I found myself lifted by some stroke of brilliant analysis or bold metaphor, frightened and spurred by acts of courage I could scarcely hope to duplicate in my life or my art. "What oft was thought but ne'er so well expressed," in women's poetry, evidently meant what had long been locked under the censor's trapdoor and was now for the first time rushing forth into the light of consciousness and language. Gradually I became aware that I was living in the midst of a literary movement that I wanted not only to experience and join but to describe as a critic. The love came first; the effort to comprehend followed.

What I had to work from, in writing *Stealing the Language* (published in 1986), was eventually over two hundred individual volumes of poetry by women and a dozen or so anthologies. From these emerged a large but indistinct picture of the women's poetry movement in America since 1960, which slowly assumed focus. I wanted to define what was new here, what was altering and expanding the meaning of "poetry," the meaning of "woman." I needed to understand how the advent of this writing was causing the past history of literature subtly, lightly, irretrievably, to change. For as Eliot in "Tradition and the Individual Talent" so finely explains that the order of art rearranges itself whenever a genuinely original new work appears, so it must shift for larger-scale literary movements as well. The women's poetry movement, it seemed to me, was destined to produce some substantial rearrangements. But of course one senses this in one's bones long before one can say precisely what has happened.

What then is important in contemporary women's poetry? What follows from women's cultural marginality and their equivocal relation to a canon that they appropriate, resist, and transform? First of all, there is the discovery that marginality, however painful, may be artistically useful. Some linked motifs announce themselves: the quest for self-definition, the body, the eruption of anger, the equal and opposite eruption of eros, the need for revisionist mythmaking. What Adrienne Rich has called "the oppressor's language" is examined suspiciously in this poetry, along with the language's rooted dualisms: male versus female, sacred versus profane, mind versus body, public versus private, logos versus eros, self versus other, subject versus object, art versus life. Not surprisingly, the strongest women poets tend to oppose hierarchy; they like boundary-breaking, duality-dissolving, and authority-needling.

Formally and stylistically, too, there are interesting developments. I want here to sketch three of these, all of which derive from and relate to particular political issues and are, I feel, designed to subvert and transform the oppressor's language into something a little closer to the heart's desire. They are the exoskeletal style, Black English, and the feminist-communal ritual. I emphasize the matter of style because it has been claimed that the women's poetry movement is not interesting *artistically*. But new meaning in poetry is necessarily signaled by new music. When the music changes, the walls of the city tremble, says Plato. It is by a tuned listening, prior to thought and reflection, that we instinctively locate the dance of the devil's party.

≥≈

Presumably in response to our culture's identification of femininity with pliability, many of the best women poets use what I call an exoskeletal style: hard, steely, implacably ironic. This is a multipurpose device. It makes the condescending label "poetess" impossible, as it is conspicuously and exaggeratedly antisentimental. It is useful for satire and parody. It is a kind of formal shell like the armor on so many of Marianne Moore's beasts, a sign of the need for self-protection on the part of the vulnerable. Unlike Moore (or more recently Amy Clampitt), however, these poets do not pretend to be charming eccentrics. Often this style is used to challenge the neutrality of the reader, addressing a "you" who is perceived as an antagonist or lover-antagonist and whose role the reader is forced to play. Usually at the same time the style implicates the poet in the oppressive scenarios she delineates. Among the deployers of this style are Diane Wakoski, Cynthia Macdonald, Margaret Atwood, and Sylvia Plath. In Plath's "Lady Lazarus," for example, the suicidal poet addresses the doctor who has restored her to life:

> I am your opus,
> I am your valuable,
> The pure gold baby
> That melts to a shriek.
> I turn and burn.
> Do not think I underestimate your great concern.[3]

Note the language play by which "opus" mocks the world of art, "valuable" the world of commerce and commodity, and "pure gold baby" reduces both to the level of vulgar hype. Note too the rhyme, in the service of contempt and self-contempt. Plath is, as women are trained to be, a commodity, an act, an exhibitionist doing "the big strip tease." She is perhaps the female object in a male poem—perhaps one of those poems like *The Divine Comedy* or Wordsworth's Lucy poems in which she has to die first. She is perhaps Galatea in the shaping hands of Pygmalion. She is passive and compliant as someone who is truly feminine should be. The "you" of "Lady Lazarus" is in the first instance a kind of sleazy sideshow manager, then becomes "Herr Doktor . . . Herr Enemy," and finally that ultimate source and rationale for male cultural authority and control, "Herr God, Herr Lucifer." As Blake's Urizen compounded the qualities of Milton's rationality-obsessed God and Milton's heaven-exiled Satan, so Plath's supreme being is perfectly evil because he is perfectly good. Plath has begun "Lady Lazarus" by describing her skin as a Nazi lampshade and her face as a "featureless, fine / Jew linen." Critics who dismiss the Holocaust imagery of this poem as childish self-aggrandizement or self-pity fail to notice its identification of a historical and political evil with ahistorical and cosmic masculine authority, and the uncomfortable collapsing of good and evil into each other. Marjorie Perloff has argued that Plath "had really only one subject: her own anguish and longing for death. To a degree, she camouflaged this narrowness by introducing political and religious images. . . . But since the woman who speaks throughout *Ariel* hates all human beings just as she hates herself, her identification with the Jews who suffered at Auschwitz has a hollow ring."[4] The hatred and self-hatred in *Ariel* (certainly in "Lady Lazarus") is palpable enough. But far from concluding that this fact invalidates the poem's metaphor of self-as-Jew, I would argue to the contrary that the combination of anger and self-hatred within victimized individuals and classes, including women and including Jews, is a universal human pattern of precisely the sort poets must explore. Note, too, that when a critic wishes to ignore the political dimension of a woman poet's work, the usual strategy is to assert that the work is "really" purely personal.

The "you" being hissed and snarled at in "Lady Lazarus" is also ourselves, her readers. Plath's portrait of the female artist as self-destroyer locks us inside a universe of concentric spheres of victimization in which we are invited if not compelled to recognize our complicity. To read is to occupy a position not unlike that of Milton's God. We are superior, remote, omniscient, judgmental, able to call the poet into life by picking up her book, able to "peel off" her disguises by critical examination. But of course Plath shares our complicity. For if this poem is a critique of control—who is more controlled than this artist? Plath's style, here and in much of her late work, brilliantly represents precisely what it despises; that is its genius, and it is the genius in a great deal of angry women's poetry.

è&

Women's poems are not of course necessarily written from within the dominant literary language. A powerful resource for poets lucky enough to have access to it is Black English, with its repertoire of cadences and phrases lifted from field hollers, spirituals, gospel, and blues on its musical side, as well as the King James Bible, high-energy preaching, and verbal rituals like rapping and the dozens on its oratorical side. The artful mimesis of "uneducated" speech has been a strategy of social criticism since *Huckleberry Finn,* first because it lets us enjoy the pleasure of breaking school rules (we all know in our hearts that rules are in the service of the rulers; to obey them is to accede to social structures for which grammatical structures are the gateway), second because it pits lively imagery against dry abstraction, humor against precept, the play of improvisation and the body's rhythms against the strictures of prior form.

Compare, for example, both Elizabeth Bishop and Lydia Yellowbird with the dry wit of June Jordan in "Poem About My Rights." Jordan is angry that she can't "go out without changing my clothes my shoes / my body posture my gender my identity my age," recalls that in France "if the guy penetrates / but does not ejaculate then he did not rape me," and "if even after smashing / a hammer to his head if even after that if he / and his buddies fuck me after that / then I consented," and proceeds to elaborate the connection between rape and imperialism:

they fucked me over because I was wrong. . . .
which is exactly like South Africa
penetrating into Namibia. . . .
and if
after Namibia and if after Angola and if after Zimbabwe
and if after all of my kinsmen and women resist even to
self-immolation of the villages and if after that
we lose nevertheless what will the big boys say will they
claim my consent?[5]

Without the unpunctuated rhythm, the combination of street-talk and authority-speak, without the legal-military "penetrate" next to the idiomatic "big boys," we would have a weaker poem. Again, in "The Rationale, or She Drove Me Crazy," Jordan composes a bravura piece with a surprise ending. The speaker in this poem is telling it to the judge:

"suddenly there she was
alone
by herself
gleamin under the street lamp. I thought
'Whoa. Check this out? Hey, Baby! What's
happenin?' I said under my breath.
And I tried to walk past but she was lookin
so good and
the gleam and the shine and
the beautiful lines of her
body sittin out there
alone
by herself
made me wild. I went wild. But
I looked all around to see where her
owner / where the man in her life could
probably be. But no show. She was out.
By herself. On the street:
As fine, as ready to go as anythin you could
ever possibly want to see so
I checked out myself: what's this?
Then I lost my control: I couldn't resist.
What did she expect? She looked foreign
besides and small and sexy
and fast

by the curb. So I lost my control and
I forced her open and I entered
her body and I poured myself
into her
punpin for all I was worth
wild as I was
when you caught me
third time apprehended
for the theft of a Porsche."[6]

Surprised? The obvious moral here is that a woman out alone is no more "asking for it" than a car asks to be stolen. A deeper point is that the poem's joke works as well as it does because our history leads us to think of women as property. As they used to say in the Gothics, he was burning to possess her, his dark-eyed beauty. But this point couldn't be made without Jordan's tuned ear. These are highly seductive rhythms, and the real secret of the poem is the poet's Shelleyan ability to put herself in the place of a bad black dude, in order to let us put ourselves there, hearing that voice of self-justification in our own heads.

What else can it mean to be an outlaw, in language and ideology? For a less violent but no less incandescent effect, here is Lucille Clifton's "Admonitions," quoted in full:

> boys
> i don't promise you nothing
> but this
> what you pawn
> i will redeem
> what you steal
> i will conceal
> my private silence to
> your public guilt
> is all i got
>
> girls
> first time a white man
> opens his fly
> like a good thing
> we'll just laugh
> laugh real loud my
> black women

children
when they ask you
why is your mama so funny
say
she is a poet
she don't have no sense[7]

The music here will be inaudible to readers for whom gender
and race are political issues but maternity is not. But as feminist
theory has for some time noticed, ours is a culture in which
psychology and literature alike represent "mother" not from
the maternal but from the child's (usually the son's) perspec-
tive. Maternal autonomy, sexuality, and conflict are conse-
quently suspect; a mother is "good" insofar as she selflessly
devotes herself to her offspring. Another consequence is that
maturation of both male and female children in our culture is
supposed to depend on rejection of the mother, identification
with the father. A third, so pervasive that we scarcely recognize
its absurdity, is the privatization of maternity: the mother's role
is a domestic not a public one. She is a being whose love for her
children must in no way impinge on society's power to dispose
of these children as it chooses.

Contemporary women poets writing as mothers—includ-
ing, for example, Alta, Susan Griffin, Adrienne Rich, Audre
Lorde, Marilyn Haeker, Marilyn Krysl, Toi Derricotte, Sharon
Olds, Marie Ponsot, Maxine Kumin, Rita Dove, Sharon Dou-
biago, Minnie Bruce Pratt, and myself, to name a few—have
come to challenge our social assumptions regarding maternity.
Additionally, they tend in describing mother-child relation-
ships to propose a profoundly antiheroic view of human power
and need. What if we stopped assuming that to be powerful
means to require worship and obedience? What if we imagined
that it might mean the ability to participate in pain and joy?
What if Milton's God, and the authorities modeled on his paren-
tal design, looked a bit more like Lucille Clifton? She tutors her
children in defiance instead of obedience; is unafraid of her
sons' lawlessness, her daughters' sexuality, and her own lack of
conventional dignity. Her first two stanzas connect class war,
gender war, and racism in the framing context of an opposed

principle of maternal affection. Her final stanza connects maternity to poetry, and both to play, with a casual impropriety that suggests a contest already won. "Noble" has been changed to "no bull," as Williams promised, but the charm and unpretentiousness of Clifton's voice increases its radicalism. Clifton's insouciance is of a similar order to Blake's, born of anger, love, and the confidence of ultimate victory. Or, as Ida Cox used to sing, "Wild women don't worry, / Wild women don't have the blues."

All these poems operate in a sense by being bilingual, negotiating between the dominant language and a marginal one, employing particularly provocative versions of what Nancy Miller calls "the irreducibly complicated relationship women have historically had to the language of the dominant culture" and what Rachel Blau DuPlessis calls the "both/and vision" of women's writing.

ed.

The poems I have cited (and feminist poems typically) have in common an "I" whom readers will find intensely engaged and engaging (or, as the case may be, enraging), aligned with the feminist conviction that the personal is the political. The poems defy divisions between public and private life because they recognize that such divisions promote oppression; a corollary is that neither poet nor reader can occupy a neutral literary space like Bishop's in "Brazil, January 1, 1502." To render a centuries-old pattern of political violence with the clarity of a tapestry but without an appearance of personal engagement is one legitimate political strategy; to pursue transformation through the poetic implication of the self is another.

A comparable logic lies behind the phenomenon of the ritual poem in feminist spiritual circles—that is to say, a poem intended to be performed, or to evoke an imagined performance, in a ceremonial setting. The primary intention of such poetry is to strengthen a sense of group or communal identity and commitment; it may or may not simultaneously critique the dominant culture and its rituals. The poet in ritual poetry enacts a bardic, shamaness' or priestess' role, enacting a modern version of the theme of transformation common to tribal ceremonies in ancient Europe, Britain, America, and Africa; she may or may not also play the part of the self-examining individual we expect literary poets to be, since the notion of the isolated artist is for many poets a tired cliché. For poet and reader-participant alike, ritual poetry implies the possibility of healing alternatives to dominance-submission scenarios. It suggests nonoppressive models of the conjunction between religion and politics, usually by re-imaging the sacred as immanent rather than transcendant, by defining its audience as members of a potentially strong community rather than as hopelessly lonely individual victims, and by turning to nature (seen as sacred and female) as a source of power rather than passivity. The language of ritual poetry, as it approximates chant, foregrounds recurrent sounds and rhythms, the sensuous qualities of words, as against their referential qualities—or, as Julia Kristeva would have it, the semiotic above the symbolic. In this way, too, it withdraws from the logocentricity we associate with the oppressor's language and approaches the pleasurable condition of the mother tongue.

The writers of ritual poetry include black poets like Audre Lorde, Ntozake Shange, and Sonia Sanchez; Native American poets like Paula Gunn Allen, Wendy Rose, Carole Lee Sanchez, Joy Harjo, and Chrystos; Third World women like Sylvia Gonzalez and Jessica Hagedorn. African goddesses, voodoo, Spider Woman, and other emblematic spiritual beings already figure widely in these poems much as Zen eminences inhabit the writing of an earlier generation of white males who needed to find or invent a sacred space from which to critique both sacred and secular institutions of the dominant American majority. Unsurprisingly, ritual poetry has received little attention from feminist academic circles, which are not themselves exempt from either racism or logocentricity, although this neglect may diminish as the excellence of "minority" women's poetry in America makes itself increasingly felt.

The imagination of female sacredness coincides with the critique of language, and both are seen as necessary conditions for political change in Judy Grahn's "She Who," a poem sequence written in 1971–72 that has subsequently become a lesbian-feminist classic. The opening section of "She Who" reads like glossolalia; a polyrhythmic set of repetitions imitates the noise of liturgical question and response, the noise of a congregation or the wind, and the naming of a goddess who might be anywoman:

> She, she SHE, she SHE, she WHO?
> she-she WHO she-WHO she WHO-SHE?
> She, she who? she WHO? she, WHO SHE? . . .
> She SHE who, She, she SHE
> she SHE, she SHE who.
> *SHEEE   WHOOOOOO*[8]

If we compare this with, say, "Who is the king of glory? . . . The Lord of Hosts, he is the king of glory," at least one crucial distinction is Grahn's funniness. As in Blake's *Marriage,* fun is a method of resisting the culture's identification of the sacred with hierarchy and command. More important, the passage cannot be read solely with the eye. It requires the voice, the participation of the body, at which point we find that Grahn's sounds and rhythms (try it, reader) are both difficult and catchy. Succeeding sections of "She Who" cover much familiar (and some unfamiliar) feminist territory—the life cycle of a woman's body, her powerlessness as an object in society and culture, her potential for power and pleasure—in a succession of formal experiments full of wordplay, teasingly disrupted syntax and narrative line, and, above all, hand-clapping and foot-tapping rhythms:

> a fishwife a cunt a harlot a harlot a pussy
> a doxie a tail a fishwife a whore a hole a slit
> > (SW, "The enemies of She Who call
> > her various names")

> am I not crinkled cranky poison
> am I not glinty-eyed and frozen. . . .
> are you not shamed to treat me meanly
> when you discover you become me?
> (SW, "plainsong from an older woman to a younger woman")

Most of "She Who," like most feminist writing, is preoccupied with struggle. Its final section, a catalogue of sixty-one women, shifts from the defensively dual to the expansively plural as in Whitmanesque fashion it invites us to be large and contain multitudes:

> the woman who carries laundry on her head
> the woman who is part horse
> the woman who asks so many questions
> the woman who cuts somebody's throat. . . .
> the woman who eats cocaine
> the woman who thinks about everything
> the woman who has the tatoo of a bird
> the woman who puts things together
> the woman who squats on her haunches
> the woman whose children are all different colors. . . .
> When She-Who-moves-the-earth will turn over
> When She Who moves, the earth will turn over.

This move toward a litany—a chant of possible selves, a vision of multiplicity as revolutionary—at present remains a marginal gesture within a marginal literature. Women inclined toward mysticism tend to make such gestures more easily than women inclined toward social realism, and those who write outside the literary and academic establishments more readily than those inside. Marginality helps liberate the imagination; Grahn's "She Who" is sister to Blake's devil.

I enjoy the gesture, the opening. My students enjoy performing "She Who" at the close of a semester. I believe that, as Luce Irigaray says in "When Our Lips Speak Together," to recognize the claims of plurality is to make hierarchy defunct: "You/I: we are always several at once. And how could one dominate the other?"[9] At its most radical, women's poetry begins to ask that question.

NOTES

1. Elizabeth Bishop, "Brazil, January 1, 1502," *The Complete Poems* (New York: Farrar, Strauss and Giroux 1969), 106.

2. The quotation is from Lynda Koolish, *A Whole New Poetry Beginning Here: Contemporary American Women Poets*, 2 vols. (Ann Arbor: University of Michigan Press 1981), 179.

3. Sylvia Plath, "Lady Lazarus," *The Collected Poems,* ed. Ted Hughes (New York: Harper and Row 1981), 246.

4. Marjorie Perloff, "Sylvia Plath's 'Sivvy' Poems: A Portrait of the Poet as Daughter," in *Sylvia Plath: New Views on the Poetry,* ed. Gary Lane (Baltimore: Johns Hopkins University Press 1979), 173.

5. June Jordan, "Poem about My Rights," *Passion: New Poems, 1977–1980* (Boston: Beacon Press 1980), 87.

6. Jordan, "The Rationale," *Passion,* 11–12.

7. Lucille Clifton, "Admonitions," *Good Times* (Brockport and New York: Boa Editions Ltd. 1969).

8. Judy Grahn, "She Who," *The Work of a Common Woman: The Collected Poetry of Judy Grahn, 1964–1977* (New York: St. Martin's Press 1978), 77.

9. Luce Irigaray, *This Sex Which Is Not One,* trans. Catherine Porter with Carolyn Burke (Ithaca, N.Y.: Cornell University Press 1985), 209.

Loving Walt Whitman and the Problem of America

I. "The poem of these States . . ."

It is a question of who is to be master. Who among the poets is to define the American character. Whitman the exuberant Emersonian contender, Longfellow the genteel Tennysonian whose *Hiawatha* appeared in the same year as the first edition of *Leaves of Grass,* or Poe, that obsessional Christopher Marlowe of the American Renaissance, decadent while yet in bud. I imagine this question must have troubled them all. Whitman at any rate reminds us constantly, in a dozen different ways, of his yearning to influence posterity. To touch it intimately. To *be* there. Exceeding the vaulting ambition of Shakespeare's sonnets, his lines announce not merely the poet's intention to achieve poetic immortality, but the intention to make his identity inescapable, his poem ubiquitous. Look for me under your boot-soles. I sound my barbaric yawp over the roof of the world. I'll be good health to you and filter and fiber your blood. Under, over, and inside. Can't get away from the man. What he assumes, you shall assume. Whitman's extraordinary verbal embrace is a far cry from the cool confidence of "My love shall in my verse ever live young," closer to Keats's "This living hand," though on a larger scale.[1] But who, what, is signified by the "you" in Whitman? Isn't that pronoun as mysterious and fluid as his "I?" To read the poem of "these States," you the reader must be you the American. He'll

From *The Continuing Presence of Walt Whitman: The Life after the Life,* ed. Robert K. Martin (Iowa City: University of Iowa Press, 1992).

explain to you, brother, sister, what that means. Using whatever material is to hand, he'll make the myth and enlist you.

An oscillation between the self defined as individual and the self defined as a portion of a collective is one part of the myth. "Myself I sing, a simple separate person, / Yet speak the word Democratic, the word En-Masse." A corrolary is the ostentatious break with high culture. Whitman's patriotism is such that he decides never in his poetry to allude to foreign literatures or philosophies, deviating sharply here from Emerson. Indeed, he avoids literary allusion altogether. "Make no quotations and no reference to any other writer," he commands himself in a notebook. "Do not go into criticism or arguments at all." To his readers he announces, "No one will get at my verses who insists on viewing them as a literary performance, or attempt at such performance, or as aiming mainly toward art or aestheticism." So radical a stance perplexes scholarship. For how can we capture between journal covers a major literary figure who pretends literature doesn't exist? Or mocks our critical acumen ("Have you felt so proud to get at the meaning of poems?") and tries to slip what he calls "the origin of all poems" past our guard, like some engaging fast-talking salesman at our door? When we literary people have accomplished a great deal of reading, we like the world to know it. But as Paul Zweig demonstrates in *Walt Whitman: The Making of the Poet,* we have in Whitman an omnivorous and obsessive reader who successfully disguised his literacy.

At the same time, Whitman loves adapting bits of foreign vocabulary and idiom, magpielike, much as the American language itself does, and sticking them in his nest. He likes the notion of poetry as universal solvent. Zweig quotes the charming naïveté of the notebook:

No two have exactly the same language, and the great translator and joiner of the whole is the poet. He has the divine grammar of all tongues, and says indifferently and alike, How are you friend? to the President in the midst of his cabinet, and Good day my brother, to Sambo, among the hoes of the sugar field, and both understand him and know that his speech is right.[2]

Later, "Song of the Answerer" elaborates on the idea that the poet speaks across class, race, occupational and ethnic boundaries, enabling all to claim him as their own. He makes his culture over into his own image, or vice versa. Expansive, bulky, soaring unbounded or out-of-bounds, he refuses a fixed hegemonic center (just as there exists no American cultural equivalent of London or Paris or Rome, but only regional cities of diverse character) or hierarchy of persons (no king, no nobility, no gentry, no breeding) or values (I am the poet of evil as well as of good) or gender (I am of the woman as well as the man). In sum, no privilege. No preference for this over that. Like America he is a poet of space, not time. Or rather, time for him is always time present and future. Cut off from those immensely overpaid accounts of Europe, he offers no valid account of the past. We cannot go to Whitman for a sense of history. The genealogical claim ("Born here from parents the same," etc.) falls flat both poetically and as effective American mythmaking, whereas the humorous roominess of "I effuse my flesh as air" or "I find I incorporate gneiss" feels authentically spacious. Even his bullying is tonally American, the bullying of a huckster. "He is an exceeding great stench," Ezra Pound remarks, "but he *is* America."

Walt gets to be America because he wants to so badly and tries so hard. Or at least he ties for first place with Emily Dickinson, that dark horse he could not have known was even in the race. Emily, who claimed she did not read him but had heard he was disgraceful. Emily, who whispers "I'm nobody" at just the moment when Walt is booming that he celebrates himself and sings himself, and that what he assumes, we shall assume. The neutrino Emily, who appears to have no mass, moves at the speed of light, and can pass through granite without reaction, might yet survive the mountainous Walt. But for the century succeeding his death, if poetry's definition of America exists, it is his. He jetted the stuff that makes Allen Ginsberg say, "America after all it is you and I who are perfect not the next world. / . . . It occurs to me that I am America / I am talking to myself again." His egalitarianism in general, and his powerful and ironic passages on slavery and the auction block in particular, make June Jordan celebrate him as the great progenitor of black, Hispanic, working-class writing:

> What Walt Whitman envisioned we, the people and the poets of the New World, embody. . . . New World does not mean New England. New World means non-European; it means new, it means big, it means heterogeneous, it means unknown, it means free, it means an end to feudalism, caste, privilege. . . . New World means, again, to quote Walt Whitman, "By God! I will accept nothing which others cannot have their counterpart of on the same terms."[3]

From "All truths wait in all things" it is scarcely the turn of a page to "No ideas but in things," and Williams's beleaguered defense of American concretion against European abstraction. More startlingly, Whitman influences mandarin as well as marginal poets. T. S. Eliot, who "had to conquer an aversion to his form, as well as to much of his matter," might conceivably never have come upon the form of "The Love Song of J. Alfred Prufrock," or the *donnée* of the speaker as the walker in the city, or the address to an indeterminate "you" at the opening and close of that poem, were it not for the example of Whitman. The austere genius of Wallace Stevens, as he begins to formulate the idea of order, imagines the bard's presence:

> In the far South the sun of autumn is passing
> Like Walt Whitman walking along a ruddy shore.
> He is singing and chanting the things that are part of him,
> The worlds that were and will be, death and day.
> Nothing is final, he chants. No man shall see the end.
> His beard is of fire and his staff is a leaping flame.

The Europeanized Ezra Pound makes a grudging pact with him and calls himself "a Walt Whitman who has learned to wear a collar and dress shirt." For Hart Crane he is of course "our Meistersinger." But to multiply instances is absurd. One should simply observe that the twentieth-century American long poem, with its fracturing of narrative and of traditional meter

("To break the pentameter, that was the first heave"—E. P.), derives as clearly from *Song of Myself* as all previous European epic derives from Homer. And when we turn, as poets, to the state of the nation and of our common life, the ghost of Whitman turns with us. Adrienne Rich argues that "the true nature of poetry" is "the drive to connect, the dream of a common language." Anthony Hecht, gesturing toward President Kennedy's asassination, can say that "we were there, / We suffered, we were Whitman." The poet of the Body and the poet of the Soul has made himself everyone's proper property.

II. "There was a child went forth . . ."

Why have I never before written about Walt Whitman? I always identify myself to audiences as Whitmanic, and I have written about Blake and Ginsberg, who are important to me but surely not more important than Whitman. Perhaps it is because I read Whitman earliest and completely outside of school. We must of course have had "O Captain My Captain" in school, and I must have hated it. My parents' Untermeyer anthology contained "Afoot and light-hearted I take to the open road," and I rather liked the swing of that. How "Song of Myself" fell into my hands I cannot say. What I remember is reading that poem straight through for the first time, when I was thirteen, outdoors amid some uncut grass. During the same year I decided Poe was mechanical, a puppet of a poet, all theatrical tricks, all indoors. This Whitman was a living creature, someone alive as I felt myself to be alive.

The location was not a meadow. I was a city girl sitting among grass and rocks in Manhattan's Central Park, where a scrim of forsythia announced April and the smell of dirt mingled with dog droppings. But the girl is mother of the woman; some portion of myself paused ecstatically at the moment when I (when it) encountered "Song of Myself" and elected thenceforth to celebrate itself and sing itself. Obviously those were the instructions conveyed by every line in the poem, for every atom belonging to the poet as good belonged to me. To read Whitman was to experience self-recognition.

Here were the self's not-yet-articulated perceptions of reality, its not-yet-formulated ideological biases, which plainly inhabited me already because I was American. Or because I was a grandchild of Russian-Jewish immigrants? Or because I was young? The generosity of spirit meant that Whitman's energies could be mine if I chose. Like some improbably open-minded parent, he would permit everything.

ða

He permitted love. That was the primary thing I noticed. The degree and quantity and variety of love in Whitman is simply astonishing. At thirteen I did not yet know the word "eroticism," much less "auto-eroticism," but I could tell when I encountered it, how each manifestation was delicately, systematically supporting all the others, like the network of filiations Whitman would later describe as spinning from the poet-spider's essence. Affection for one's own body, "that lot of me and all so luscious," "no sweeter flesh than sticks to one's own bones," underwrote the will to incorporate material phenomena—"all this I swallow, it tastes good, I like it well, it becomes mine"—the love of the world, the spectacle of other people, but also the love of what Whitman named the soul. Thus it was with ravishment that I read the amazing section 5 of "Song of Myself":

> I believe in you, my soul, the other I am must not abase itself
>   to you,
> And you must not be abased to the other.
>
> Loafe with me on the grass, loose the stop from your throat,
> Not words, not music or rhyme I want, not custom or lecture,
>   not even the best,
> Only the lull I like, the hum of your valved voice.
>
> I mind how once we lay such a transparent summer morning,
> How you settled your head athwart my hips, and gently turn'd
>   over upon me,
> And parted the shirt from my bosom-bone, and plunged your
>   tongue to my bare-stript heart,
> And reach'd till you felt my beard, and reach'd till you held
>   my feet.

Swiftly arose and spread around me the peace and knowledge
    that pass all the argument of the earth,
And I know that the hand of God is the promise of my own,
And I know that the spirit of God is the brother of my own,
And that all the men ever born are also my brothers, and the
    women my sisters and lovers,
And that a kelson of the creation is love,
And limitless are leaves stiff or drooping in the fields,
And brown ants in the little wells beneath them,
And mossy scabs of the worm fence, heap'd stones, elder,
    mullein and poke-weed.

Though the temptation is simply to sigh, let me unravel something of what the green thirteen-year-old self must have apprehended in these lines. For the passage is a microcosm of Whitman's poetic method at its best . Outrageously elusive play is its essence. Describing (inventing) a scene (or fantasy) of masturbation, or of lovemaking with another person, or of mystical communion—if it is impossible to tell which, the point is that such scenes are interchangeable and equivalent, just as "I" and "the other I am" and "you" stand in poised balance. The point is also that Whitman makes it humorously impossible to locate the relation of parts to whole, for each takes on the qualities normally assigned to another. "I" in this passage seems at first a kind of genial arbiter between "my soul" and "the other I am" (presumably the body), those famously rivalrous but insecure siblings. But the relationship immediately shifts. As soon as "I" invites an encounter with "you," "the other I am" disappears before it is even defined. If this term was to stand for "body," why was Whitman not more explicit? Was it to make body echo the cryptic self-identification of God to Moses in Midian, "I am that I am"?[4] In section 4 the mysterious entity "I am" was an observing ego. Now in section 5 if "you" is still "my soul," Whitman is clearly redefining the soul as seperable from and equal to the self (instead of a portion of it); as nontranscendant, nonhierarchical; as in fact possessing *its own* body capable of relaxing, and its throat capable of humming. Whatever Western philosophy from Plato through protestant Christianity has made of the soul, Whitman radically bypasses. Nor can one assimilate this image very easily to Emerson's

Oversoul. All that remains here of any notion of an immaterial essence is the sequence of cultural negatives that Whitman wishes away and the "stop" he wishes loosed. "Only the lull I like, the hum of your valved voice," with its seductive assonances, proposes a soul like the drone of Indian music, a vibrant fulness that is also void; "lull" would be a sound something like a lullaby, along with a cessation of movement.

More melting takes place during and after the long four lines describing the lovemaking between self and soul. "I mind" seems a relaxed idiomatic equivalent of "I recall" or "I remember," while allowing "mind" to register almost as a substantive noun. The "transparent" morning prepares us for perceptions and acts that will meet no obstacle. The future implied by the ego's invitation shifts to a recalled idyllic scene in which both self and soul are physically embodied, as if "the other I am" were diffused between them or distributed among them. For the work of Eros, which is to join whatever is disconnected, requires palpability; vision is not enough. The tacit action behind the described lovemaking resembles that in Donne's poem "The Ecstasy," where the lovers mingle ("interinanimate") first their souls, then their bodies:

> So must pure lovers soules descend
> T'affections, and to faculties,
> Which sense may reach and apprehend,
> Else a great Prince in Prison lies.
> To'our bodies turn we then, that so
> Weak men on love reveal'd may looke;
> Loves mysteries in soules do grow,
> But yet the body is his booke.

Like Whitman, Donne wants to mediate the quarrel between body's impurity and soul's purity. The crucial difference is that soul and body remain logically distinguished and hierarchically conceived by Donne, whose theology requires the inferiority of bodies to souls, even while he boldly compares physical lovemaking to the Incarnation. It is exactly that logical and hierarchical conception that Whitman opposes and rejects, in every inflection of his writing, as false.

The ego's penetrability in this passage provides one element of its sweetness. There is something wonderful, always, in such moments of ecstatic male surrender. One feels it in Keats, often, and in Wyatt's "They Flee from Me," when the lady enters his chamber:

> In thin array, after a pleasant guise,
> When she me caught in her arms long and small:
> Therewith all swetely she did me kiss
> And softly said, "Dere hert, how like you this?"

Another element is the musicality, the assonance of "settled . . . head . . . gently" tied to the alliterated "head . . . hips," the plosives of "*p*arted my shirt from my *b*osom-*b*one, and *p*lunged your tongue to my *b*are-stri*p*t heart," the off-rhyme of "shirt" and heart," and above all the deep sound of "lull" and "hum" transformed to "plunged your tongue." Meanwhile the easy roll of mixed iambs and anapests, with the feminine endings of the first two lines, collects toward the successive stresses of "báre-strípt héart" and the tight, stretched, monosyllabic last line, with its long *e*'s reinforcing the tension: "reach'd . . . beard . . . reach'd . . . feet."

Several particulars are important in Whitman's description of orgasm. "Swiftly arose and spread" marks the contrast after the sequence of iambs and anapests; the long line enacts the sensation of expansive ripples, and "of the earth" suggests their extent, while "pass all the argument" conflates the sense of "surpass" with a suggestion that "argument" is static compared with the motion of peace and knowledge. Eros makes waves. But they are halcyon waves. The peace and knowledge that pass all the argument of the earth are what T. S. Eliot also invokes in the triple "Shantih" at the end of "The Waste Land," glossed as "the peace that passes understanding." Yet from Whitman's perspective, Eliot's fear and loathing of sexuality would make samadhi unattainable. We might also contrast what happens in this passage with the climax of Emily Dickinson's "Wild Nights! Wild Nights!" another poem of autoerotic and androgynous fantasizing that uses the idea of a wide space of water, but then brings it to closure in contraction instead of expansion:

Rowing in Eden -
Ah, the Sea!
Might I but moor - Tonight -
In Thee!

For Whitman the pull toward safety and enclosure never occurs. Instead, the rest of this passage dissolves the conventional division between sexual and mental gratification, returning us to a biblical sense of what it means to "know," without sin, or grief, or loss of self. Knowledge is cosmic and inclusive then subsides, as the orgasmic sensation gently ebbs, back to perception of the physical environment. That environment is itself emblematic of sexuality, being "limitless" and including phallic leaves ("stiff or drooping") and vaginal earthy declivities ("wells") full of insect life, finally declining to weedy textural particularities.

During this process—as the reader may not notice—time past has returned to time present, and the "you" has disappeared from the description along with "the other I am." The soul as lover, as active partner, has been, as it were, reabsorbed into the self—was the reaching and plunging a beginning of this reabsorption?—and has emitted waves of peace and knowledge, much as the fusion of two atoms produces radiation. By the close of the passage even the assertive repetitions of "I know" are gone, absorbed in their turn into the living minutiae of what is known.

Now, section 5 of "Song of Myself" either is or is not an objective correlative for the reader's erotic experience. There I was, a palpitating adolescent, reading poetry to myself in the park as I so often did, with the noises of dogs, children, a softball game, in my circumference and airplanes periodically overhead—and it seemed to me Whitman had it just right. He had me. He was me. Myself in the slippery moment when I was able to fall in love with anything, beautiful boys, hunched elderly women, frisky dogs, cerulean clouds above Fifth Avenue, mica in the sidewalk, softball teams. Writers commonly remain loyal to the enthusiastic creatures they are in adolescence. I hold dear the child that was simmering, simmering, simmering, and was brought to a boil, given permission to exist by "Song of Myself." For decades afterward the activity of writing poetry seemed to me essentially erotic, as Whitman repeatedly insists it is. Poetry aroused me bodily, felt at once passive and active, derived from an unarguable consciousness of the vitality and beauty of the world, and rested on a conviction that what I could feel, see, know, in states of excited joy, was real. The erotic was not "sex." It had nothing to do with conquest. It was a means of knowledge.

III. "Through me forbidden voices . . ."

When a girl becomes a woman, and discovers her disadvantaged cultural status, Whitman's presence may strengthen her incalculably. Both for my own poetry and for the poetry of many other American women, Whitman has been the exemplary precursor, killer of the censor and clearer of ground. Even his crudest statements on gender, the insistence in "Song of Myself" that "I am the poet of the woman the same as the man," or his equal-time advocacy of male and female bodies in "I Sing the Body Electric," are revolutionary compared with the sentimental conventions of his own time. I suspect they are still revolutionary compared with the psychoanalytic doctrines that pass for valid utterance about gender and sexuality today. The poet H.D., under analysis by Freud in the 1930s, struggled painfully uphill before she could write "woman is perfect":

> herself
> is that dart and pulse of the male,
> hands, feet, thighs,
> herself perfect,

in the poem entitled "The Master." But Whitman had already considered the topic of anatomy and concluded, "That of the male is perfect, and that of the woman is perfect," adding of the female form that phallic "mad filaments, ungovernable shoots play out of it," much as he noticed at sunrise that "something I cannot see puts upward libidinous prongs." He had already addressed "you workwomen and workmen of these States" in "A Song for Occupations." His Adam had already imagined his Eve "by my side or back of me . . . or in front, and I following her."

But what moves me, and I suspect other American women poets, is less the agreeable programmatic utterances than the gestures whereby Whitman enacts the crossing of gender categories in his own person. It is not his claim to be "of the woman" that speeds us on our way, but his capacity to be shamelessly receptive as well as active, to be expansive on an epic scale without a shred of nostalgia for narratives of conquest, to invent a rhetoric of power without authority, without hierarchy, and without violence. The omnivorous empathy of his imagination wants to incorporate All and therefore refuses to represent anything as unavailably Other. So long as femaleness in our culture signifies Otherness, Walt's greed is our gain. In him we are freed to be what we actually are, in whatever portion of ourselves eludes society, system, and philosophy: not negative pole to positive pole, not adversarial half of some dichotomy, but figures in an energetic dance. His sacralization of sexuality anticipates the black poet Audre Lorde's widely read feminist manifesto "The Erotic as Power." The phallic economy of which feminist theorists complain has no place in a diffuse polymorphous eroticism whereby the aggression supposedly proper to adult males yields to "that lot of me and all so luscious." Whitman's evocations of "touch" align him with female celebrants of tactile intimacy from Anne Sexton, who cries that "touch is all," to Luce Irigaray, who argues that feminine pleasure depends upon touch as masculine pleasure depends upon the gaze. Above all, the woman in Whitman speaks to us through his impulse to question boundaries—to prefer fluidity to fixity, experiment to status quo. If women poets in America have written more boldly and experimentally in the last thirty years than our British equivalents, we have Walt to thank.[5]

&

I do not mean to say that Whitman is a man for all feminist purposes. He solves the problem of marginality by denying the existence of a center, transforming the figures of self, nation, cosmos, into a vast flood plain of sensations, affections, filiations. For him there is no outsider position, hence no dilemma of powerlessness. High and low, rich and poor, slave and free, are all for him actors in a pageant. Such a solution is beautiful but useless to the slave. Whitman can write splendidly and deeply of death; he can write powerfully and glancingly of pain and doubt; he cannot write at all about chronic fear, anger, defeat, despair. Happily independent of institutions, including that of marriage, he has no sense of what it means to be crushed by them. His ubiquitous identification of "woman" with maternity is profoundly reductive, as is his identification of "negro" with "slave." Were there no free blacks roving Mannahatta in whom Walt might have rejoiced? He may have flattered himself that "forbidden voices" spoke through him, but if those voices had protest in mind, if they had anger to vent, if they thought to organize politically, Walt was no trumpet of prophecy to them. If we want a nineteenth-century poet in whom the desire for power and the fact of powerlessness remain inescapably knotted, we turn to Emily Dickinson. Emily, whose poems are theaters of war, saturated in the language of politics. The poet who writes, around 1864, "Peace is a fiction of our Faith."

IV.
"No longer let our children deem us riches and peace alone, We may be terror and carnage, and are so now."

A taste for violence, even to self-destruction, appears to be as permanent an attribute of our species as the need for food or the craving for sex. Oh, give me an enemy, give us an enemy, give—! A bliss in proof, and proved, a very woe. But who knows how to shun the heaven that leads men to this hell? Writers, mirroring humanity to itself, have flung the brutal realities of war before our faces for thousands of years, not omitting the excitement, the keenness. To hurl oneself irrationally into scenes of fatal violence: why would anyone do it? The answer, my friend, is blowing in the verses of Homer and Virgil, the Bible, Shakespeare, and Whitman as well.

Whitman's enthusiastic support of the Civil War might have been predicted from the eroticism at the core of his early work, just as Pound's mature fascism grew from the proto-fascism of his early poetry, with its strutting, its hero worship, its intolerance. Although like most northerners Whitman despised slavery, he thought the abolitionists were crude fanatics and would never have made the mere end of slavery a casus belli. No, like Lincoln's, his theme was Union. This great, sweating, fragrant body of work—Whitman's art—dedicates itself to Union. Union on a continental scale signified what the manly love of comrades signified socially and the amorousness of soul and body with the "Me Myself" signified psychologically. That the States should adhere—not cohere but *adhere*— was essential. The preservation of Union, in Whitman's view, was worth any sacrifice. Therefore the Civil War brought Whitman tragic joy. All this he tasted, it became him.

It is typical of Whitman that his Civil War poetry contains no animosity or belligerence. He eschews crude partisanship: "Was one side so brave? The other was equally brave." "My enemy is dead, a man divine as myself is dead." Like William James, he is aware that war excites and delights people regardless of ideology. A "shock electric" runs through Manhattan at the outset of conflict. The drums and bugles thrill. The flag and pennant hymn seductively of "Demons and death . . . and a pleasure new and ecstatic," to which the poet answers, "You undulate like a snake hissing so curious, / Out of reach, an idea only, yet furiously fought for, risking bloody death, loved by me, / So loved—." The artilleryman safe at home dreams a battle scene with cannon "rousing even in dreams / A devilish exultation and all the old mad joy in the depths of my soul." When he found his vocation as hospital visitor, nurse, and spiritual "wound-dresser," ultimately ministering to the needs of nearly a hundred thousand sick and wounded soldiers on both sides, Whitman's compassion was matched by his realism, his homoerotic gratification by horror:

> From the stump of the arm, the amputated hand,
> I undo the clotted lint, remove the slough, wash off the
>   matter and blood,

boundaries of separation, as always implicitly erotic, always a form of making love.

Making love. Poetry. An odd combination. In postmodern, media-drenched America, eros equals pornography, both for its advocates and its attackers. Or else it equals possession, a consumer product. Many poets, and almost all critics, avoid it (except in the special category of AIDS writing, where eros equals mortality). What most contemporary critics seem to want is less body and less feeling in poetry. Less sensuousness. Less desire—these topics are so sticky, so embarrassing, so impolite, so troublesome—can't we, please, have a poetry that's *clean*, with the messy and horrifying fluids and emotions scrubbed off it?

Not that academic disapproval of eros is new. Freud properly observed that libido is precisely what socialization represses. Yeats rhymes entertainingly on the scandalousness of poets to pedants: "Lord, what would they say / If their Catullus walked that way?" The passage I have quoted from Sir Philip Sidney suggests that the topic of love was slightly unacceptable to the scholarly mind at the very moment when Europe and England were being flooded with love sonnets. Modernist poetics, insofar as it pursues the ideal impersonality recommended by T. S. Eliot, or bows to Pound's distaste for "emotional slither," constitutes an apex of anerotic sublimation—however undermined by the practice of poets like Frost and Williams. It is no coincidence that the only one of the major women modernists to be respectfully canonized was the sexually respectable Marianne Moore, while the deviantly sexual H.D., Loy, and Stein, not to mention conventionally amorous lyricists like Millay, were snubbed by the boys' club of the New Criticism. His impassioned and explicit exploration of the erotic is among the many causes that keeps Robinson Jeffers in critical limbo, a potential embarrassment. In our own time, too, in the wake of the "confessional" poets, there seems to be a backlash of critical opinion emphatically preferring the abstract to the sensuous, the cerebral to the emotional. In part for this reason, the austere poetry of Elizabeth Bishop is universally praised and the physically and sexually charged poetry of Sharon Olds commonly attacked. I have seen these attacks in print, heard them at conferences; the detractors never, of course, say that Olds's poetry hits too close to home or is too emotive or too sexual for their taste; they never say that it makes them uncomfortable. Certainly not; the disparagement is always on purely aesthetic grounds. (*Aesthetics:* one notices that those who invoke the term most loftily from the comfort of the citadel can seldom say what they mean by it. It is the outsiders swarming the barricades who are forced to formulate definitions.)

I have just been reading a much-discussed volume of academic criticism by Vernon Shetley, *After the Death of Poetry*,[1] and find myself itching for a quarrel. Beyond the provocative and exasperating title, Shetley is no fool but a rather subtle, sensitive, and ingenious reader. It is perfectly clear that he loves poetry and some poets. He concludes an encomiastic chapter on Elizabeth Bishop with a kind of gratuitous coda describing Sharon Olds as a "representative mainstream poet" who fails to live up to the Bishop tradition. What is this about? Why put Olds in the same bin as Bishop in the first place? The oddness of it makes me think. My own view is that Shetley's elaborate discussion of Bishop is skewed toward the erasure of eros in her poetry, that his sniffy dismissal of Olds derives from a horror of eros in hers, that he misreads both, and that his misreadings are entirely typical of academic criticism. I want to argue—an argument triggered by Shetley, whom I take (since I too need a scapegoat) to be a representative mainstream critic—that, notwithstanding apparently polar differences between Bishop and Olds, including where they locate themselves on a continuum of erotic desire and dread, the two poets share an understanding of what eros *is*.

II.

> Why, why do we feel
> (We all feel) this sweet
> sensation of joy?
> —Elizabeth Bishop, "The Moose"

The qualities Shetley praises in Bishop are familiar ones. He admires her reticence, her withholding of meaning, her "reluctance to moralize or draw conclusions," and the closures that pose "undecidable alternatives"—though with a new twist. These qualities have, he claims, acquired greater resonance since our present knowledge of Bishop's unhappy childhood and her lesbianism enables us to perceive what the poems function to conceal. A votary of "difficulty," Shetley demonstrates that Bishop employs figures of similitude (simile, metaphor, implied analogy) throughout her career to express or imply *un*likeness, *dis*similarity, skepticism regarding the possibility or desirability of connection. Under the banner of postmodernism, he admires, in other words, Bishop's resistance to the erotic.

Shetley's discussion concentrates on four poems. In "The Monument," he claims, Bishop, like Eliot, implies a poetics of "artistic impersonality as a defense against painful personal history." Attributing life to an artifact is "a means of evading questions of human agency . . . the poet can conceal himself behind the objecthood of the artwork." "The Weed," a counterpoem of the creative moment, appears to recoil from its narrative of fertility, variety, and motion. Covertly, the poem "explores the uneasy territory of feeling associated with the fear of and revulsion from pregnancy." "At the Fishhouses" extends these anxieties regarding the female body to anxieties about the poet's relation to a female-coded nature and a looming maternal sea. Lastly, "In the Waiting Room" is read as describing a "fall into connectedness" that can only be experienced as horrifying.

These strong and persuasive readings add up to a plausible account of the force of alienation in Bishop as a postmodern poet.[2] Shetley's picture coincides, moreover, with the view of astute critics like Bonnie Costello, who notes Bishop's "impersonal mode" and "variety of distancing techniques," or Robert Pinsky, who asserts that Bishop "saw the world with . . . preternatural clarity in order to distinguish herself from it."[3] Yet all such readings omit something crucial, which in each case touches on the erotic potential of *likeness*. It is this erotic potential, however guarded and oblique, that I hope to recover. To put it another way, I want to suggest how needy Bishop's texts are, how variously they reach toward tenderness, connection, communication, touch, how armored and veiled that neediness is—lifting only at moments in the late poems—and yet how impossible it is to imagine Bishop as a poet of the isolated autonomous self.

Of the four poems Shetley discusses I will discuss two, one from the beginning and one from the close of her career. "The Monument," one of Bishop's earliest poems on the problematics of art, takes the form of an implied dialogue between an insistent instructor and a resistant pupil (who might also stand for two halves of a self or two theories of art—one sophisticated and one naive). The instructor addresses a "you" who is, however, never personally spoken to; the speech concentrates on its "object" as if illustrating the very principle of objectivity:

> Now can you see the monument? It is of wood
> built somewhat like a box. No. Built
> like several boxes in descending sizes
> one above the other.
> Each is turned half-way round so that
> its corners point toward the sides
> of the one below and the angles alternate.
> Then on the topmost cube is set
> a sort of fleur-de-lys of weathered wood,
> long petals of board, pierced with odd holes,
> four-sided, stiff, ecclesiastical.[4]

While the speaker's attention shifts from the monument's geometry toward its possibly "melancholy or romantic" intentions, its need "to cherish something," its relation as artifact to nature, and its fuction of sheltering "what is within," which may or may not be the artist-prince's invisible bones, the questioner remains stubbornly literal:

> "Why does that strange sea make no sound?
> Is it because we're far away?
> Where are we? Are we in Asia Minor,
> or in Mongolia?"

Where Shetley along with most with other critics privileges the former's aesthetics and scorns the latter's naive and irritable queries, an equal and opposite reading is also possible. We can see the instructor as pompously insensitive to the personal needs of the questioner, and the poem as a wry mockery of how aesthetic and academic pretentiousness crush human tenderness. When the questioner, sulking like a child or like anyone who's been dragged to do something educational and uplifting, says, "Why did you bring me here to see it?" the instructor, like many an authority figure, refuses to respond. From the instructor's point of view, discourse is appropriately monologic. Aesthetic discourse excludes "you" or "me." But what if the poem, unlike the instructor, invites us to take both sides of its frustrated dialogue seriously and personally?

In that case we must yearn along with the questioner for personages and art objects less abstract and more tender, while yearning along with the instructor for a student better able to appreciate the unseen behind the seen. As a genuinely dialogic poem about the value of culture, "The Monument" subtly anticipates the reversals of Adrienne Rich in "Snapshots of a Daughter-in-Law," with its ironic responses to poetic passages by Horace and Campion, as well as suggesting a companion piece to Stevens's "Anecdote of the Jar," with its nature/artifact dialectic, or "The Idea of Order at Key West," with its assertions and unanswered questions as well as its peninsular setting. Or perhaps Bishop's poem is a wry deflation of the monumental magnificence in Yeats's "Sailing to Byzantium." One might trace all five of these poems back to Keats's "Ode on a Grecian Urn," where the opposition of art to life, and the identification of that opposition with the stasis of ever-unfulfilled "happy love" versus the rot and decay of fleshly sexuality, is made explicit. Again, if "The Monument" projects onto visual art the problem of inferring subjectivity from the object, and achieving intersubjectivity in aesthetic dialogue, it constitutes a rejection (determined? sad? resigned?) of Whitman's promise:

> Have you practis'd so long to learn to read?
> Have you felt so proud to get at the meaning of poems?
> Stop this day and night with me and you shall possess the
>   origin of all poems. . . .
> You shall no longer take things at second or third hand. . . .

> You shall not look through my eyes either, nor take things
>   from me,
> You shall listen to all sides and filter them from your self.

None of what Whitman offers is possible in the world of "The Monument," yet to read the poem fully is to experience that impossibility as a genuine loss.

Neither speaker in "The Monument," curiously, is gendered. Either might be of either sex. What is gendered—gendered and classed—is the hypothetical creator, an "artist-prince" whose theorized motives explicate the monument's paradoxically gimcrack appearance. Gendered as well is the artifact itself, a "stiff, ecclesiastical" sort of phallus from which four slanted "poles spring out . . . like fishing-poles or flag-poles," from which in turn "jig-saw work hangs down" in "four lines of vaguely whittled ornament . . . to the ground." A wooden ejaculation, then, that poignantly reveals itself as "having life, and wishing . . . to cherish something" but also rather comically "may be solid, may be hollow." By the poem's close, the instructor shifts from speculating on the artifact's past to proposing that it has a future:

> It is the beginning of a painting,
> a piece of sculpture, or poem, or monument,
> and all of wood. Watch it closely.

To watch is to anticipate motion, but nothing in the poem permits us to know whether motion will or will not occur, whether the absurd effigy lives. We have been teased out of thought, as with Keats's "cold pastoral," but in place of romantic epiphany is postmodern discomfort. If refined aesthetic perception and speculation requires and/or produces human impersonality, "The Monument" permits us to feel both the necessity and the terrible pity of that remoteness. It is a poem of deep and disappointed yearning.

A vastly different poem from "The Monument" is Bishop's late masterpiece "In the Waiting Room." Opening her last published volume, *Geography III,* its voice is that of a child of almost seven, who sits reading the *National Geographic* on a winter evening in a crowded dentist's waiting room while waiting for an aunt. The magazine contains photos of a volcano's "inside . . . full of ashes" and in eruption, and some primitive women whose "breasts were horrifying." Suddenly, "from inside"—the second time this word appears in the poem—the child hears a cry of pain. She identifies the voice at first as her aunt's and then with surprise as her own, coming from her own mouth: "Without thinking at all / I was my foolish aunt, / I—we—were falling, falling." When she tries to remind herself who she is, disorientation increases: "I felt: you are an *I*, / you are an *Elizabeth*, / you are one of *them*," and the unanswerable question surfaces: "*Why* should you be one, too?"

> I knew that nothing stranger
> had ever happened, that nothing
> stranger could ever happen.
> Why should I be my aunt,
> or me, or anyone?
> What similarities—
> boots, hands, the family voice
> I felt in my throat, or even
> the *National Geographic*
> and those awful hanging breasts
> held us all together
> or made us all just one?

For Vernon Shetley and other critics, this "fall" into identity with others is experienced as repellent. Shetley remarks how disagreeably mediocre and ordinary the other people in the poem are. Yet part of what the child Elizabeth intuits and the adult Bishop implies is that the emergence of a self-conscious individual identity can never be separable from an experience of identification with others. The child has heard a voice "from inside," and we discover along with her that "inside" may be something external or may be something hidden within one's own throat. What emerges from inside is the unacknowledged, irrational universal, described here as "a cry of pain that could have / got loud and worse but hadn't," registered by the suddenly emergent "I." Identity, the having and being an "I," is what separates me from all others, and also what unites me with them. Is it also what saves me from "worse"? Does it save Bishop from identifying too fully with her mad, forever-lost mother? Self *is* self-in-relation: no other kind exists.

Or, perhaps, no other kind exists for women. For a whole literature has lately come into existence arguing that the construction of self as self-in-relation is gendered female, while the self as autonomous is gendered male.[5] Applying this principle to culture as well as to individuals, androcentric criticism unsurprisingly tends to promote conceptions of the detached individual, to disparage representations of affectional relationships as sentimental, and to read poems like "In the Waiting Room" as expressions of terror and disgust at one's place in a human community. But if we are tempted to think that the mysterious "similarities [that] held us all together / or made us all just one" can only be disgusting, we forget the alternative. As the child returns to ordinary consciousness, she notes that "the War was on." War, in this poem and all Bishop's work beginning with "Roosters," epitomizes the egoistic sublime of lives, and nations, that cannot perceive themselves with due modesty and due empathy as "just one."

If Bishop both yearns for and fears the erotic, experiences it as actual or potential pain, and produces screens to disguise the experience, we as readers need not be equally shy. We may let ourselves see the ubiquity and ambiguity of intimacy in Bishop, noting its obliquely imagined presence in the figures of "The Map," its teasing affectionateness in "Invitation to Miss Moore," the surreally articulated pain of its absence in poems like "The Man-Moth" and "Insomnia," its tentative consummation in "Shampoo," and numerous unfinished or unpublished explicit love poems in Bishop's notebooks. "Love should be put into action!" screams the old hermit in "Chemin de Fer," shooting off his shotgun in crazy confirmation of desire, or loneliness, or perhaps masculinity, early in Bishop's career. But she herself could never put it into such direct poetic action. As many commentators have noticed, several poems in *Geography III,* published in 1976 at a high-water mark of the women's poetry movement from which Bishop distanced herself, approach to a certain extent the personal openness that was a hallmark of that movement. "In the Waiting Room" is one such poem. Another is "Crusoe in England," which uses the persona of the male castaway to articulate intense loneliness and longing—and hint shyly at homoerotic tenderness in the portrayal of Friday, "Pretty to watch; he had a pretty body." A third, "The Moose," locates the speaker in a night bus en route from Nova Scotia to Boston, swathed half-asleep in the murmurings of passengers that collectively exemplify the cycles of village life, interrupted by a female moose who sniffs at the bus, looks and is looked at. "Why, why do we feel / (we all feel) this sweet / sensation of joy?" Is the moose a figure for the missing mother, returned from "the impenetrable woods," now "safe as houses" yet also "grand, otherworldly?" Is it this imagined return that allows Bishop so confidently and uniquely to state a collective joy? "The Moose" contrasts sharply with Frost's "The Most of It," in which an isolated male self fails to achieve "counter-love, original response," from the buck who represents wilderness. Here, a relaxed acceptance of communal sensibility enables the further recognition that what we joyfully recognize in nature is ourselves.

For many readers the signature poem of Bishop's late period is the villanelle "One Art," a tour de force of form and a stellar instance of rhetorical indirection. The power of "One Art," and its closing confession, which stumbles so tellingly over the almost untellable fact of love—

> —Even losing you (the joking voice, a gesture
> I love) I shan't have lied. It's evident
> the art of losing's not too hard to master
> though it may look like (*write* it!) like disaster—

lets us know how difficult, and how central, love was to Bishop's art: to *write* it, without writing it, was a lifelong task.

III.

> But I have this,
> so this is who I am, this body

> white as yellowish dough brushed with dry flour
> pressed to his body. I am these breasts that
> crush against him like collapsible silver
> travel cups . . .
> > if you
> want to know who I am, I am this, *this*.
> > —Sharon Olds, "This"

Nobody would say Sharon Olds disguises the erotic in her poems. The erotic in her work is ubiquitous, joining bodies of flesh, generations, natural cycles of procreation and decay, human to animal, animal to vegetable, male to female, profane to sacred, life to art, sex to food to writing. The title poem of Olds's first book, *Satan Says,* announces the program of her art. Trapped inside an ornamental box she is trying to "write [her] way out of"—her childhood, her body, a sentimentalized tradition ornamented by tacky shepherds—she is tempted by Satan to escape by saying things like "fuck" and "shit" and cursing her parents; she obeys, but as the lid of the box opens and she is about to exit into Satan's mouth, she remembers "I loved them too," and the lid closes. The poet will remain locked in the box that is now her coffin, but she hardly cares, as freedom to articulate rebellious hate precipitates "the suddenly discovered knowledge of love."[6] Olds chooses to be a poet ambivalently but firmly attached to parents. Several other poems about writing in this first volume announce corrolary facets of her agenda. In "Nurse Whitman," Whitman's and Olds's love of men is at once compassionate and sexual, embodied and imagined, while a fusion of present and past joins a fusion of genders in an act of writing that is also an act of conception and birthing:

> We lean down, our pointed breasts
> heavy as plummets with fresh spermy milk—
> we conceive, Walt, with the men we love, thus, now,
> we bring to fruit.

In "The Language of the Brag," a poem that follows several poems describing the intensely absorbed animal life of "Young Mothers," Olds asserts the act of childbirth as a "heroism" equivalent to phallic power ("I have wanted excellence in the knife-throw. . . . the haft slowly and heavily vibrating like the cock") and to the creation of poems. Having lain down and passed blood, feces, water, and a new person covered with "language of blood like praise all over the body" into the world,

> I have done what you wanted to do, Walt Whitman,
> Allen Ginsberg, I have done this thing,
> I and the other women this exceptional
> act with the exceptional heroic body,
> this giving birth, this glistening verb,
> and I am putting my proud American boast
> right here with the others.

That the poems are intended to be both transgressive and sacred is made clear. "Station" describes the poet's husband, left to mind the children while she writes, gazing at her with "the poems / heavy as poached game hanging from my hands." "Prayer," the final poem in *Satan Says,* defines "the central meanings" through linked images of copulation and childbirth, closing with a Whitmanlike vow: "let me not forget: / each action, each word / taking its beginning from these."

Whereas Bishop writes as a voice of loneliness, fearing and desiring connection, the self in Olds is never represented in isolation but always in relation, penetrated and penetrating, glued by memory and gaze to others. She scandalously eroticizes the bodies of children and parents, genitals and all, describes the sex act with explicit attention to a variety of orifices, is obsessed with the foodlike and procreative possibilities of human bodies, loves images of animals, soil, blood, and eggs, represents her sexually greedy body as a tiger's, an anteater's, that which "takes him in as anyone in summer will / open their throat to the hose held up / hot on the edge of the sandlot," and insists "I am this, *this*." Cross-gendered imagery recurs through her work, as she invokes "my father's breasts" or speculates that her mother made her deliberately in the image of the powerful father: "I feel her looking down into me the way the / maker of a sword gazes at his face in the steel of the blade." Sperm is recurrently described as milk, sexual gratification as eating and drinking, sex as power: "The center of your body / will tear open, as a woman will rip the / seam of her skirt so she can run," she tells her daughter. Olds's sacralizing of the sexual and procreative body is sometimes explicit, sometimes textually hinted, as when the daughter's maturing body is described as rising bread in a way that half-represents the girl as Christ.

Olds's critics complain at times that she sensationalizes the dysfunction of her natal family—cold, alcoholic grandfather and father, searingly clinging anorexic mother—overlooking the complication of the daughter's insistently expressed desire for, worship of, and identification with the father's body, which persists throughout her recent volume about his dying and death. The sensuous profusion in Olds stands in stark contrast to the austerity of a writer like Bishop. Some readers conclude that such rich surfaces cannot possibly coexist with depth. Yet there may be important unsaid, unsayable, matter in Olds just as there is in Bishop. Consider "Sex Without Love," the single Olds poem that Shetley discusses, which he claims uses metaphor merely ornamentally:

> How do they do it, the ones who make love
> without love? Beautiful as dancers,
> gliding over each other like ice-skaters
> over the ice, fingers hooked
> inside each other's bodies, faces
> red as steak, wine, wet as the
> children at birth whose mothers are going to
> give them away. How do they come to the
> come to the come to the God come to the
> still waters, and not love
> the one who came there with them, light
> rising slowly as steam off their joined
> skin? These are the true religious,
> the purists, the pros, the ones who will not
> accept a false Messiah, love the
> priest instead of the God. They do not
> mistake the lover for their own pleasure,

they are like great runners: they know they are alone
with the road surface, the cold, the wind,
the fit of their shoes, their over-all cardio-
vascular health—just factors, like the partner
in the bed, and not the truth, which is the
single body alone in the universe
against its own best time.

The poem's opening "How do they do it?" may be con-
strued as wondering either about technique or about morality.
The question lets us know that the speaker *doesn't* do it, but
not whether she envies or deplores. The following swift succes-
sion of similes implies a slippage from admiration—what we
might feel if our ideas of sex without love came from watch-
ing, say, James Bond movies—to something closer to horror
or pain. Sex without love is attractive in the style of art or
sport, athletically and socially attractive, then it is a bit like the
hanging carcasses in a Frances Bacon painting, then it paral-
lels food, then for a brief instant it shockingly resembles the
most shameful abandonment of the helpless.

Significantly, Olds does not dwell on this instant, although in
another poem ("The Abandoned Newborn") her topic is the
condition of an infant left wrapped in plastic in a dumpster.
The simile nonetheless jars and reverberates, for the mother-
infant image simultaneously connotes and negates the vulner-
able and utterly satisfied infantile eroticism that we strive to
retrieve in adult sexuality (several other Olds poems also make
this connection). The line break reinforces the poignance of
expectation dashed, the full stop signals a dead end along one
line of thinking. At the edge of the image, or our consciousness
of it, especially if we happen to be mothers ourselves, might be
the fact that *all* mothers (including the mother of Jesus, who
was Love) give their babies away, if not sooner then later. The
pain of this abandonment is not accidentally but systematically
a corrolary of a culture in which sexual pleasure is divided from
procreation and motherhood is sentimentally honored but in-
stitutionally disempowered and without status. It is, in other
words, a real *effect* of "sex without love." Shetley's comment on

this simile calls it "entirely gratuitous; since babies whose mothers are going to give them away are exactly as wet, no more and no less, as babies whose mothers are going to keep them, this elaboration serves no purpose but to remind us that sex without love may lead to unwanted pregnancy, a message better suited to public service announcements than poetry." Both tone and content of a sentence like this suggest to me a reader deeply out of touch with his topic.

Shetley fails to comment on lines 8–13, in which the speaker cannot quite articulate what sex *with* love is. But this is the core of the poem. "Come to the   come to the   God" works doubly. It stumbles over the inexpressible and exclaims over its own inarticulateness, much as Bishop stumbles and exclaims in "One Art." It also half-implies that what love "comes" to is, precisely, God. "Still waters" reinforces and deepens this implication while echoing and redeeming the wetness of sexuality and of the newborn. Each a pool from which the other drinks, we taste a shared water of life. Sex, the speaker suggests, brings us to the pastoral oasis of the Twenty-third Psalm, our animal innocence, our divine protection. It restores our souls. Loving whoever comes to such a space with us would itself be natural. Sex, birth, nature, innocence, God, and a revisionary rereading of scripture are all involved here. The image of light rising like steam from the lovers' "joined skin" imaginatively turns the fact of perspiration into a signal of the holy. The experience lies, however, outside the poem's discourse: the poem offers a silence that the reader must fill in.

And the remainder of the poem appears to repudiate or transcend the oasis experience. Loveless lovers know better, we are told: they don't make the mistake of substituting the priest (the sexual partner) for the god (the pleasure). The true religion of eros is strenuously self-absorbed; the extended final metaphor of sex as running against one's own best time (one's own best orgasm) insists on our absolute isolation.

Shetley's comment on Olds's "Sex Without Love" calls its metaphors "descriptive rather than cognitive." Clearly they have not made *him* think; the assumption that women who write about sex must be brainless is a very old one, which I've documented elsewhere. His commentary concludes as follows:

Ultimately, the poem's challenge to conventional values, both sexual and poetic, is recontained through the distance and isolation in which the poem envelops these in some sense unimaginable persons. The poet professes to admire these exemplars of lucidity. . . . But ultimately, [she] consigns them to their aloneness, professing her incomprehension; she . . . prefers to remain within the emotive comfort of false beliefs. By the poem's end, its initial challenge to conventional values of emotional warmth and mutuality has been entirely defused.

An intelligent critic has to be gripped by some blinding anxiety to read a poem this poorly. Olds's "in some sense unimaginable persons" certainly exist and sometimes might be any of us; the poet initially professes incomprehension but in the end undertakes to explain them quite convincingly. Far from resting in the comfort of "conventional values of emotional warmth and mutuality," which the critic apparently identifies with "false beliefs," the poet recognizes the equal and opposite reality of those who make sex without love. More interesting is that the sharp, best-case understanding of the loveless lovers whom she continues to call "they" means the speaker simultaneously is and is not like them. Is it that her empathy overrides and invades their loneliness, in order to understand their experience from within? Or is it, rather, that their perfect and superior loneliness rebukes and explodes her empathy? Two kinds of lovers, two concepts of God, two ontologies of self, constructed as "undecidable alternatives" not unlike those we admire in Bishop, govern this poem. And while it is an atypical poem for Olds because it does not use the first-person singular, it is typical in its capacity to represent sexuality as both desirable and frightening.

Now let me ask two questions. What sort of erotic discourse do Bishop and Olds share? And can we correlate this sharing with anything in their rhetorical habits as poets? The first question can be answered rather simply. Bishop mostly evades, Olds mostly asserts erotic connection—but for both, the erotic is a power preceding and defining the self; for both, it exists at the liminal border between language and the unsayable; for both, it abuts on a realm we may call spiritual. Technically, however cool the voice of Bishop, however seemingly overheated the voice of Olds, the metaphors of both poets enact the erotic.

Olds's do so, as I hope I have shown, first of all by their excess, which is mimetic of the procreativity Olds identifies with eroticism; second, by requiring us constantly to register interplays of likeness and difference across categories, and in particular by repeatedly collapsing the categories of the human, the natural, the divine, and the artistic while reminding us of their conventional separation. To say "I am this," and mean the body, is in Olds to claim complete connection with the world.

Bishop's metaphoric technique works differently and so subtly that one of her most characteristic and unique strategies has scarcely been noticed. From the beginning to the end of her work, Bishop has a habit of letting metaphor attribute life and motivation to the inorganic, humanity to the inhuman. In "The Map,"which begins Bishop's first published volume, "These peninsulas take the water between thumb and finger / like women feeling for the smoothness of yard-goods" In her final published volume, the final poem, "Five Flights Up," posits a dog and bird querying the day and knowing "everything is answered, / all taken care of" by the day—radically unlike the speaker.

Because Bishop's tone is always conversational, whimsical, modest, we perhaps fail to notice her passion for violating categories, joining the separated. "Somebody loves us all," she remarks humorously at the end of "Filling Station," attributing to an unknown other what is really an attribute of her own imagination. Perhaps she comes closest to self-reflection on this attribute in "Santarém," with its dappled opening of "houses, people, and lots of mongrel/riverboats skittering back and forth" at the conflux of the Tapajós and Amazon Rivers:

> I liked the place. I liked the idea of the place.
> Two rivers. Hadn't two rivers sprung
> from the Garden of Eden? No, that was four
> and they'd diverged. Here only two

and coming together. Even if one were tempted
to literary interpretations such as: life/death, right/wrong,
    male/female
    —such notions would have resolved, dissolved, straight off
    in that watery, dazzling dialectic.

First comes liking, then speculative analysis and a self-correction implying that this scene of lively anarchy and confluence is rather better than Eden, and an emphatic disavowal of dualistic abstractions. The joining of the rivers is a quiet and delightful metaphor for all conjunctions of supposed opposites amid the dazzling play of variegation.

In a very early poem, "Casabianca," Bishop tells us that the boy who stood on the burning deck, obstinately and stammeringly "trying to recite 'the boy stood on the burning deck' . . . while the poor ship in flames went down," is Love: "and love's the burning boy." If Bishop alludes simultaneously to the child god Eros and to the incarnate Jesus, she is doing no more than was done by the seventeenth-century devotional poets she so admired. Robert Lowell, though he admired Bishop, thought "Casabianca" trivial. But the Song of Songs tells us, as Bishop would have known, that many waters cannot quench love. One hopes not even the discomfort and incomprehension of critics in an age of intellectual drought can do that.

NOTES

1. Vernon Shetley, *After the Death of Poetry* (Durham, N.C.: Duke University Press, 1993).
2. Reasons for Bishop's resistance to the erotic are not far to seek: loss of a mother to madness, self-censorship regarding lesbianism, internalization of a moral training that stressed control, the stigmatizing of sexuality in women poets, and so on. Everyone recalls how Bishop had to take a stand against her mentor Marianne Moore's disapproval of "water-closet" in "Roosters." Less well-known is the fact that the first more or less explicit love poem Bishop tried to publish, "The Shampoo," was turned down by both *Poetry* and the *New Yorker* and politely ignored by friends. I am indebted to Victoria Harrison, *Elizabeth Bishop's Poetics of Intimacy* (Cambridge: Cambridge

University Press, 1993), 70–73, for pointing this out. This kind of hushing continues in the ostensibly liberated 1990s. Reviewing Robert Giroux's edition of Bishop's letters, Adrian Oktenberg remarks that Bishop appears in it as "a woman almost without libido," despite her love affairs with Lota de Macedo Soares and others, and pertinently asks, "is Bishop the only poet in the history of the world never to have written a love letter?" (*Women's Review of Books* 11, nos. 10–11 [July 1994]: 28).

3. Bonnie Costello, "The Impersonal and the Interrogative in the Poetry of Elizabeth Bishop," in *Elizabeth Bishop and Her Art*, ed. Lloyd Schwartz and Sybil P. Estess (Ann Arbor: University of Michigan Press, 1983), 109; Robert Pinsky, "Elizabeth Bishop, 1911–1979," *New Republic*, November 10, 1979, 255.

4. Citations of Elizabeth Bishop's poetry in this essay are from *Elizabeth Bishop: The Complete Poems, 1927–1979* (New York: Farrar, Straus and Giroux, 1992).

5. Among the key works arguing this position are Dorothy Dinerstein, *The Mermaid and the Minotaur: Sexual Arrangements and the Human Malaise* (New York: Harper and Row, 1977); Nancy Chodorow, *The Reproduction of Mothering: Psychoanalysis and the Sociology of Gender* (Berkeley: University of California Press, 1983); Carol Gilligan, *In a Different Voice* (Cambridge: Harvard University Press, 1982).

6. Citations of Sharon Olds's poems are to *Satan Says* (Pittsburgh: University of Pittsburgh Press, 1980); *The Dead and the Living* (New York: Knopf, 1984); *The Gold Cell* (New York: Knopf, 1987); *The Father* (New York, Knopf, 1992).

Making the Connection
The Nature Poetry of Maxine Kumin

I.

Our genes declare themselves
—"The Knot"

Which of her poetic peers does Maxine Kumin resemble? A little later in this essay I hope to show that Kumin's nature poetry is unlike anyone else's, and it may help to begin with her indelibly sane stance as a woman and feminist living and writing in a country setting. Unlike Sylvia Plath and Anne Sexton, she keeps her demons bridled. Unlike Elizabeth Bishop or May Swenson, who remained cautiously reticent in the work they published during their lifetimes, she can be intimately and even bawdily personal. Like Adrienne Rich, she makes us pay respectful attention to images of strong female identity, to issues of family life, and to questions about our relationship to the earth, yet she avoids the systematically ideological. The yoke of her tutorials is light, glinting with humor and rue.

Perhaps the gender wars should leave us all feeling like the walking wounded, but Kumin seems to be—dare one say it—comfortably heterosexual. It may well be that Western civilization stands in crisis, shortly to be doomed. The animals are going under as well, species by species, occasionally with the

From *Telling the Barn Swallows: Poets on the Poetry of Maxine Kumin,* ed. Emily Grosholz (Hanover, N.H.: University Press of New England, 1997).

help of well-meaning human intervention. But Kumin avoids the apocalyptic mode. True enough, as the title poem of her 1982 volume of *New and Selected Poems* reminds us in an extended conceit on airports and lifespans, our ground time here will be brief.[1] But Kumin prefers to speak directly of our personal and common mortality and only obliquely of humanity's potential to destroy and self-destruct. So, for instance, in "Getting Through" in her 1985 volume *The Long Approach,* after a lyric opening in which "the calendar of bad news" is covered over by "snow lucid, / snow surprising, snow bees . . . an elegiac snow of whitest jade,"

> Even if the world is ending
> you can tell it's February
> by the architecture of the pastures.
> Snow falls on the pregnant mares,
> is followed by a thaw, and then
> refreezes so that everywhere
> their hill upheaves into a glass mountain.

Truth is being defeated, as it were, by beauty. Thanks to the blizzard, with the phone dead and the mail and newspapers undelivered, "Bombs and grenades, the newly disappeared . . . go unrecorded," while the foals

> flutter inside
> warm wet bags that carry them
> eleven months in the dark. . . .
> If there's an April
> in the last frail snow of April
> they will knock hard to be born.

To be "in the dark" of prebirth parallels human ignorance about political terror. The two conditions are equally temporary, but the poem chooses to conclude with the probability of birth, an image of hope shadowed by the conditional "if" and by the "frail snow" that obliquely signals the frailty of all life. The close of "Getting Through" is like a pragmatic farm-woman's version of Shelley's armageddon-like "trumpet of a

prophecy . . . If winter comes, can spring be far behind?"
When you live with the weather of New England, neither
winter nor spring stands for finality, and the small births can
be allowed to balance the large deaths—though one must al-
ways hedge one's bets. Again, in "The Green Well" of *Looking
for Luck*, the daily trip to

> a kitchen midden
> where the newly dead layer by layer
> overtake the long and longer vanished

evokes memories of a dead mare ("After the lethal phenobarb,
the vet / exchanged my check for his handkerchief") and a
dead friend whose suicide still burns like betrayal. From and
through such losses, life continues:

> The cats clean themselves after the kill.
> A hapless swallow lays another clutch
> of eggs in the accessible nest. It does
> not end with us, not yet, though end it will.

"We go on" is a phrase Kumin has used more than once.
Sanity, notwithstanding tragedy, is her way. It is the way of
someone rooted in a chosen set of routines and responsibili-
ties. Kumin differs from other feminists in her capacity to
locate strength in normality. And is there another feminist
poet who finds or invents such a sweet male alter ego, a bit like
and a bit unlike herself, highlighting continuities and distinc-
tions across gender and other boundaries?

Henry Manley, the country neighbor who is one of several
recurring figures in Kumin's poems, could be the most endear-
ing animus in the business. "Last fall he dug a hole and moved
his privy / and a year ago in April reamed his well out,"
though in his dotage. Having had a phone installed, he tramps
two New England miles, "shy as a girl," to ask the poet if she'd
be so kind as to call him one day. Stricken with aphasia, Man-
ley is "as loose in his skin as a puppy" and frightened after
dark. But at dawn,

he gets up, grateful once more
for how coffee smells. Sits stiff
at the bruised porcelain table
saying them over, able
to with only the slightest catch.
Coffee. Coffee cup. Watch.

Typical of Maxine Kumin's art are the sensory weight, the play of alliteration and assonance sliding into the closing couplets, the perfectly expressive halting and crystallizing rhythms. In another poem Henry breaks his hip, is taken in by neighbors, enjoys his new role of storytelling sage. When he goes on crutches to see his old collapsing house, presently occupied by porcupines, he says, "You can't look back."

Mirroring his creator, Henry Manley is a capable country-person of multiple skills. He will die before the poet does and is one of her many means of studying mortality. Like the un-named "hermit" of *Up Country,* Henry is no macho type but a relatively feminized male whose old age makes him charm-ingly unthreatening. He is also, however, what the poet is not, or can be only through him: an *isolé.* He is alone, not looking back. In this respect his masculinity governs. For her, not look-ing back would be intolerable. What drives her poetry, slam-ming the accelerator to the floor, is attachment. If she had her way, no loved (or hated) human or animal would die unre-membered. What Kumin calls her "tribal poems," poems on family, have always formed the core of her work. The longer she writes, the more inclusive her conception of family grows. Father, mother, brothers, husband, daughters and son, great-grandfather, uncles—they are only the beginning.

"Sperm," a tragicomic celebration of seventeen look-alike cousins,

O Grandfather, look what your seed has done!
Look what has come of those winter night gallops.
You tucking the little wife up
under the comforter that always leaked feathers.
You coming perhaps just as the trolley
derailed taking the corner at 15th Street
in a shower of blue sparks

typifies Kumin's insistence that family is both biological and social phenomenon. Biology may not be destiny, but it is reality, generating "chromosomes tight as a chain gang." A sequence of poems on a beloved dying brother offers that insistence another way. In "The Incest Dream," shortly before the expected death, a grieving hangman brings the brother's severed penis, "pressed as faithfully / as a wild flower" for the poet to keep "and lie back down in my lucky shame." When the brother has died, "Retrospect in the kitchen" describes the forty pounds of plums harvested from his tree and brought three thousand miles to preserve. The making of preserves is a recurring metaphor, in these poems and in Kumin's essays, for what the poet wants to do with the world at large. Other tricks also work. People fade, but animals "retrieve" them, as the title poem of *The Retrieval System* explains. Ponies begging for apples equal two elderly aunts; a boy buried at sea reappears in a yearling's gallop; splitting logs at the woodpile simultaneously releases the soul of the beech and recalls the soul of the lost friend, Anne Sexton.

Children, especially daughters, keep cropping up, growing as they go, from Kumin's earliest work to her most recent. Though the poems commonly explore the delicate process of releasing the young ones into their own lives, "our genes declare themselves" in passionate attachment. Children have lately been joined by grandchildren, newborns with whom "Body to body my monkey-wit soaks through." Notice how in both these quotes biology is metaphorically associated with intelligence and expression, in tacit defiance of nature-culture dualisms. The maternal voice, once virtually nonexistent in poetry, has become in the last few decades one of the most significant products of the women's literary renaissance, and no poet writes more lucidly of mother-child relations. Or, for that matter, of animal-human relations, since her maternal attachment and attention extend to the forms and gestures, the detailed lives and deaths of mice, turtles, frogs, goats, beavers, cows and calves, sheep and lambs, bears, toads, dogs and kittens, interdependent sloths and moths, and—most powerfully—horses.

Creatures gravitate toward Kumin and she to them; she

tells their tales like family anecdotes; she anticipates their doom. At times, as in "Woodchucks," "How It Goes On," or "Taking the Lambs to Market," she is their doom's guilty agent. "The Vealers" invokes the single day when newborn calves may root and suckle, their ten weeks' mechanical feeding, "never enough to set them loose / from that birthday dividend / of touch," and their handing over to the knacker, whence they will emerge "wrapped and labelled in a plastic sheet, / their perfect flesh unstreaked with blood / or muscle, and we will eat." At other times, as in "Thinking of Death and Dogfood" or "A Mortal Day with No Surprises," she contemplates the uses of horseflesh and her own potential "to sweeten a crop / when the clock-hands stop" and wishes her mare and herself good endings. Yet again, she is midwife of foals, milker of cows, feeder of birds, mucker-out of barns, maker of hay, grower of vegetables.

Vegetables as well as animals, in Kumin, receive affectionately graphic attention. Pea plants "saying castanets, saying dance with me, / saying do me, dangle their intricate / nuggety scrota". A final purple cabbage in the garden is "big as a baby's head, big as my grandson's brain." "Darlings, it's all a circle," she explains in "Family Reunion," and those she addresses might be plants, beasts, or human kin. Thoreau, whom Kumin often cites, would commend her honesty, the precision of her language, her adhesion to the rituals of farm life, and her occasional moral allegory. The practical thumb more than the theoretical hymn of American nature-worship is what molds her writing, as it did his.

Whether Thoreau would approve of the emotional and sexual attachments that for her are inseperable from her attachment to nature, is another matter. An amusing swerve from Thoreau occurs in "Beans," a poem in *Up Country* not later reprinted. Recalling Henry David's boast of "making the earth say beans instead of grass," Kumin addresses a lover who keeps her weeds down and makes her say beans at his touch. The prim bachelor Henry David might not have been amused. And this brings me to the question of Kumin's uniqueness as a poet in her chosen field. Her chosen landscape, I should say, of fields, woods, barn, farmhouse, pond, garden—in which ed to be called poetic diction may have been invented precisely for the purpose of distinguishing countrified matter from dignified manner. As Dryden explains in the preface to his translation of Virgil's *Georgics,* the poet must carefully avoid "letting his subject debase his style . . . nothing, which a phrase or saying in common talk, should be admitted into a serious poem." Rather, he must clothe his theme "in the pleasantest dress that poetry can bestow upon it," with metaphors, Grecisms, and circumlocutions, to give his verse the greater pomp, and preserve it from sinking into a plebeian style."[3] To the classicist, writing nature poetry is a class act dependent on the privileging distance of aristocracy. To the romantic, who wants to avoid class privilege (or, more likely, isn't born to it), nature poetry offers access to a mode of lament, a form of rebellion, and an always-doomed attempt to return to a sacralized maternal unity that language and consciousness forbid.

When a disaffected Wordsworth complains that the world is too much with us—"little we see in nature that is ours"—nature's wildness is feminized as (among other images) "this Sea that bares her bosom to the moon," and his longed-for self is appropriately infantilized in "Great God! I'd rather be / A Pagan suckled in a creed outworn." Wordsworth's most famous evocations of a nature that nurtures man's inner self—"Tintern Abbey," the Immortality Ode, the Lucy poems, "The Prelude"—recount the same fable of loss and resignation. Shelley's impassioned cries for union with the tumultuous natural energies of skylark, cloud, wind—"Be thou, Spirit fierce, / My spirit! Be thou me, impetuous one!"—apostrophize precisely what is beyond the reach of the feeble self. Keats pursues his death-defying nightingale to an imaginary eroticized landscape from which he inevitably and forlornly wakes.

Like their English cousins, the poets of the American Renaissance often seem peculiarly remote from the nature they contemplate. Emerson's transparent eyeball sees but does not touch, and his natural world (commonly figured as maternal) is usually generalized to a transparency through which the Unitarian Oversoul manifests its disembodied glory. Thoreau boasts that he makes the earth say beans and pays scrupulous

nature, by being semi-domesticated, becomes something new and interesting in the history of poetry.

II.

nor is it one thing to save animals
and people another
but seamless
—"Caring: a Dream"

Suppose we place Kumin in the general category of "nature poets," or see her work as belonging to a long tradition of pastoral or bucolic poetry that began with Hesiod and Theocritus in Greek, Virgil and Horace in Latin. That tradition explodes in the English Renaissance with the tremendously influential poetry of Sir Philip Sidney and Edmund Spenser, includes lyricists like Campion, Herrick, and Marvell, reaches a romantic climax with Wordsworth, Shelley, and Keats, and flickers on through the Victorians as a sort of remembrance of things past in Tennyson, Arnold, and Hardy. Nature in this richly accretive tradition at times is presented realistically. Hesiod's *Works and Days* offers a versified farmer's almanac-cum-agricultural manual, gritty with the sweat of experienced manual labor; Virgil's *Georgics* describe, if from a refined distance, actual practices of farming, fishing, horse rearing, and beekeeping in first-century Rome.

More often, the natural world represents an idealized innocence of amorous or tuneful shepherds and shepherdesses, simple villagers, inspiring landscapes, mythically charged sublimities, rural retreats. The wild, the free, the spontaneous, the untamable, the refreshingly uncorrupted: Shelley's liberating west wind and the "unpremeditated art" of his skylark. Keats's nightingales, his bowers, his zephyrs. Radiating through the sublime and the beautiful are death and decay, as nature's cycles provide the inevitable setting for elegy. Milton's "Lycidas," Shelley's "Adonais," Tennyson's "In Memoriam," are among the loftier monuments of English poetry; Hopkins's "To Margaret" and Dylan Thomas's "Refusal to Mourn the Death, by Fire, of a Child in London," among the most haunting.

In America there scarcely seems a nineteenth-century poet who *doesn't* write nature poetry. Thanks to the frontier, with a little help from Whitman, America *is* Nature, as opposed to the wicked Old World that is Culture. And among twentieth-century poets we have an extraordinary number who not only write about nature but live in / on it and in a variety of ways feel called upon to defend it. Think of Frost, Jeffers, Robert Penn Warren, Theodore Roethke, A. R. Ammons, Robert Bly, Gary Snyder, Donald Hall, W. S. Merwin, Wendell Berry, to name a few.

The astute reader will have noticed that this grouping includes no women. In fact, Kumin is among a handful of women poets for whom observation and advocacy of nature are primary activities—notably herself, May Swenson, Mary Oliver. Why is this? Women and nature, according to certain tenacious cultural habits, at least in the West, tend to be confused with each other. That is to say: in the languages of literature, philosophy, and psychology (and sometimes science), nature is construed as female, and females construed as natural, therefore wild, therefore dangerous as well as desirable, requiring conquest and control. From the Greeks to the Enlightenment and beyond, the ooze of femaleness lurks and laps at the borders of male rationality, threatening rot and decay. A female chaos waits to devour a male order. "There's hell, there's darkness, there's the sulphurous pit," cries King Lear, thinking of women's nether parts, "burning, scalding, stench, consumption, fie, fie, fie"—just as T. S. Eliot, in an excised passage of *The Waste Land,* invokes "the hearty female stench."

Within Western religious discourse, from Eve to the Whore of Babylon, natural women mythically represent the aggressive and vile sexuality of an immanent Mother Nature requiring to be subdued by a transcendant Father God. The anthropologist Sherry Ortner observes that "Woman is to Nature as Man is to Culture" in numerous societies both primitive and advanced. Susan Griffin's exhaustive and brilliant *Woman and Nature: The Roaring Inside Her* pursues the analogy's encoding of power and oppression according to which males, like deities, ought to act, think, judge, speak, stare, control, possess. Females, and nature, had better be acted upon, judged,

spoken about, stared at, controlled, owned—or, hell breaks loose. Languages of authority, from to poetics, are masculine, the theorists tell us, w language remains a set of meaningless murm claims, Nature is silent.

Margaret Homans speculates that the ider women with objectified nature in men's poems obstacle to the nineteenth-century woman poet.[2] I poses of poetic tradition one *is* Nature, and ough (like a violet by a mossy stone) and be described, t possible to write *about* Nature? The problem defea Wordsworth and partly defeated Emily Brontë, a Homans; Dickinson just barely conquered it throu intense paradox and doubleness in which nothing it says. Homans's theory, with its reliance on a Lac digm in which the "symbolic order" of language rejection of nature and femaleness, has always see exaggerated; but how are we to explain the paucit nature poets? Is it not significant that Marianne Moc rate fauna, for example, are so much more textual tr

Kumin's solution—which is not to say that she c thinks of Homans's problem as a problem for her accept the identification of herself and/as nature ar rather gallop, with it, while steadfastly refusing to any order "higher" than nature or "beyond" natur side" nature. A firmly secular poet, she does not my the natural world—it does not stand for something o itself—and with one exception, to which I will return does not personify earth as mother. Nor does she myt language, or culture, as if they were seperable from reality. Particularizing rather than generalizing, she metaphor not to *elevate* but to *articulate* phenomena double sense of expressing them clearly and showir connections and conjunctions (cf. L. *articulus,* joint). I so, it seems to me, she tacitly dismantles the philosoph psychological scaffolding upholding much of what we nize as nature poetry and simply builds on another plo

Most nature poetry actually inscribes man's alienatio nature. Court poets write pastorals, shepherds do not

attention to every detail of wood and pond. Yet one feels ever the shade of distinction between the naturalist's gaze and the object gazed at. "I am no more lonely than a single mullein or dandelion in a pasture, or a bean leaf, or sorrel, or a horse-fly, or a humble-bee," he claims. Nonetheless, to a crucial question Thoreau asks shortly thereafter in *Walden*—"Shall I not have intelligence with the earth? Am I not partly leaves and vegetable mould myself?"—the answer is mysteriously negative: "Nature puts no question and answers none which we mortals ask." In the chapter "Higher Laws," Thoreau argues for outgrowing one's "slimy beastly life" of "animal" appetites: "Nature is hard to be overcome but she must be overcome."[4] Toward the close of *Walden* Thoreau invokes a feminized nature of another sort, an elusive beloved whose attractiveness is somehow one with her cruelty:

> At the same time that we are in earnest to explore and learn all things, we require that all things be mysterious and unexplorable, that land and sea be infinitely wild, unsurveyed and unfathomed by us because unfathomable. . . . I love to see that Nature is so rife with life that myriads can be afforded to be sacrificed and suffered to prey on one another; that tender organizations can be so serenely squashed out of existence like pulp,—tadpoles which herons gobble up, and tortoises and toads run over in the road; and that sometimes it has rained flesh and blood!

Nature as femme fatale appeals to Thoreau as Other, however, not as Self. Even Whitman views nature from without, as much as he participates in it. "I think I could turn and live with animals," he says, but the device is the familiar one of pastoral satire; the poet uses the appeal of animals ("they are so placid and so self-contained") to mock the folly of humans. Whitman finds he incorporates gneiss, considers the grass to be the flag of his disposition, and would far rather be outdoors than in a stuffy drawing room, but he does not say he is himself an animal. In the magnificent "Out of the Cradle Endlessly Rocking," the mourning bird and the maternal death-whispering sea are of an alien order from the boy who will be initiated by them into poetry. "When Lilacs Last in the

Dooryard Bloomed" uses its natural images almost exactly as Milton and Shelley use theirs.

Among the twentieth-century poets, disinclined as they usually are to mythologize nature, Robert Frost can treat "putting in the seed" as something both agriculturally and humanly erotic, and represent himself as an active participant within a natural world in poems like "Mowing" and "After Apple-Picking." Yet most of the time one feels in Frost the tacit remoteness of the observer or controller of nature—a remoteness regretted, for example, in poems like "The Most of It," where nothing in the natural world returns a man's need for "counter-love, original response," or in "Never Again Would Birds' Song Be the Same," where an Adam attributes to Eve's voice the capacity to "influence" the birds ("And to do that to birds was why she came"), or "Neither Out Far Nor in Deep," where people "look at the sea" despite their inability to penetrate its essence. Similarly with poets like Ammons, Merwin, and Berry: however tenderly they love and mean to protect the world of nature, the habit of assuming that man is essentially differentiable from nature lingers.[5] Insofar as mythopoetic versions of nature haunt American poetry today, they are likely to perform the old gender functions. Williams goes from "Spring and All" (dazed virgin) to *Paterson* (blowsy female Park). We see Stevens's "Madame la Fleurie," at the close of a lifelong dichotomizing of Reality and the Imagination, swallowing her dead poet, whose "crisp knowledge is devoured by her, beneath a dew":

> The black fugatos are strumming the blacknesses of black. . . .
> The thick strings stutter the final gutterals.
> He does not lie there remembering the blue-jay, say the jay.
> His grief is that his mother should feed on him, himself and
>   what he saw,
> In that distant chamber, a bearded queen, wicked in her dead
>   light.[6]

Robert Bly's "The Teeth Mother Naked at Last" reaches as far back as Babylonian myth for an image of violence as quintessentially female. An important exception is Gary Snyder, whose adaptations of Native American and Buddhist perspectives enable him largely to shake the vertical standard whereby mind is superior to matter and spirit to nature. Not accidentally, Snyder shares with Kumin a penchant for particulars in his poems—how many Snyder poems there are with the exact place marked, the activity—and a mistrust of dualism in his philosophy. We need, Snyder says, "to look clearly into the eyes of the wild and see our self-hood, our family, there. . . . At the root of the problem where our civilization goes wrong," he continues,

> is the mistaken belief that nature is something less than authentic, that nature is not as alive as man is, or as intelligent, that in a sense it is dead, and that animals are of so low an order of intelligence and feeling, we need not take their feelings into account.[7]

Even more than Snyder, Kumin does say she is an animal. She says it again and again. She says animals are like people too, using a colloquial and anecdotal mode that is the precise antithesis of the language recommended by John Dryden, avoiding the aura of myth and sacrament cultivated by the romantics and some of the moderns, and avoiding as well their separation anxiety. When Kumin says these things, it feels perfectly normal and obvious, so that one is a little startled to remember how rarely one finds parallel moments in other poets.

"June 15" is one of the entries in "Joppa Diary," Kumin's first sequence of poems based on her New Hampshire farm experience. It is typically anecdotal, but the unpretentious diction disguises a radical poetic agenda. I quote the poem in its entirety:

> On this day of errors
> a field mouse brings forth her young
> in my desk drawer.
>
> Come for a pencil,
> I see each one,
> a wet steel thimble pulled out of its case,
> begin to worm its way uphill
> to a pinhead teat.

As if I were an enlarged owl
made both gross and cruel,
I lean closer.

The mother rears and kills.
Her forelegs loop like paper clips
as she tears at her belly fur,
shredding it fine as onion skin,
biting the blind and voiceless nubbles off.

Later, she runs past me.
I see her mouth
is stuffed full of a dead baby.

(GT 207)

Technically, I think it is important to notice, in this apparently casual poem, the veiled internal and end rhymes (*errors/drawer, pencil/steel thimble/uphill/owl/cruel/kills, loop/clips, me/see/baby*), alliterations like "wet . . . worm," "biting the blind," the assonance of "mouse" at the opening with "mouth" at the close, and the startling effect of saving the human term "baby" for the very end. More interesting and less obvious is the poem's defining balance of literal and metaphoric—"realistic" and "literary" language—and the way it effectively balances the scales between viewer and viewed. The mouse begins as an actual mouse, although "brings forth her young" has a comfortably literary sound. Then the desk-drawer images (wet steel thimble, pinhead, paper clips, onion skin) make semicomic play with the invasion of desk space by outdoor creature, while the parallel grotesque figure of poet as owl—standing for wisdom and also predation—traverses the boundary in the opposite direction. The last stanza drops metaphor completely. One remembers the Dickinson who observed that "Nature, like us, is sometimes seen / Without her diadem" and watched as a bird "bit an Angleworm in halves / And ate the fellow, raw." The refusal of sentiment in the depiction of motherhood is central for Kumin, as is the unstated lesson that our own behavior may parallel that of other mammals, but notice too the refusal of weighty symbolism. The devouring mother is not glamorized enough to be a Devouring Mother.

I have already mentioned some of the "retrieval" poems in

which animals wear the visages of lost kinfolk. The following is a representative sample of passages that make clear Kumin's crossing of species boundaries in a variety of moods. In a love poem, "we" are "two lukewarm frogs . . . our tongues at work in their tunnels / our shut eyes unimportant as freckles." In "Eyes" a woman's "grand / comedy of anguish" in front of a highball glass is like a sparrow in a hawk's hands, a monarch butterfly flailing in a gauze net. In "The Summer of the Watergate Hearings" worms in Amanda's droppings are like the parasites falling out of the government on TV. When the poet is tired, her arms "hang down simian style." Anger, in one of many poems limning the independence of children, "turns the son into a crow, / the daughter a porcupine." The poet off to teach a class on prosody, a colleague recording mockingbird imitations of cardinals, crows, and semis' airbrakes—and the birds themselves—are all working on "our single-minded imperfect song." Wild turkeys in a blizzard approach the farmhouse "like swimmers daring the deep end." April lambs keep the poet awake with "their separate baaings . . . all of us missing our mothers."

In a dream poem, "Making the Connection," the poet falling asleep hears an old dog's ghost arrive "on metal toenails," whimpering, soon to "howl in the prison of his deafness," reminding the dreamer of the dog's grim death.

> I sit up, breaking the connection,
> like hanging up on my brother.
>
> I am ten. I go down terrified
> past a houseful of bubbling breathers,
> unlatch the cellar door, go further
> down in the darkness to lie on old carpet
> next to the incontinent puppy.
> His heartbeat, my heartbeat, comfort us.

This descent to the remembered "Brother Dog" parallels the descent in Adrienne Rich's "Diving into the Wreck" and concludes similarly with a dissolving of self into Other. Women poets in quest of "the thing itself and not the myth" typically "go down" rather than surmount. The antiheroic gesture of memory and reunion subverts the male commandment to transcend. The connection is many connections: waking and dreaming, living and dying, adult and child selves, as well as human and animal siblings.

The specificity of Kumin's attachments so rarely gives way to any alternative poetic dimension of symbolism that it is worth noting one poem that comes close to personifying earth as mother—even as dangerous mother—if only to show how the poem deflects and perhaps even mocks its own Freudian paradigm. "Mud" begins by evoking a cthonic female whose simultaneous sucking and pouring threatens to overwhelm and uncreate her own cosmos:

> You would think that the little birches
> would die of that brown mouth sucking
> and sucking their root ends.
> The rain runs yellow.
> The mother pumps in, pumps in
> more than she can swallow.
> All of her pockmarks spill over.
> The least footfall
> brings up rich swill.
>
> The streams grow sick with their tidbits.
> The trout turn up their long bellies.

All sensuousness, no mind, heavily contrasted with the human world (which "would think"), this excessively mucky maternal mouth and surface closely resembles Thoreau's "slimy beastly" appetites and the happily destructive Nature who "must be overcome," or Stevens's "bearded queen." A long array of formless maternal monsters in English literature, including Spenser's Error and Milton's Sin, similarly gorge and spew their own substance.[8] But by the end of Kumin's "Mud," after the evocation of slugs, of "an army of lips . . . in its own ocean," and of boulders giving birth to rocks, something different happens:

> Meanwhile the mother is sucking.
> Pods will startle apart,
> pellets be seized with a fever
> and as the dark gruel thickens,
> life will stick up a finger.

The surprise is that the blind, formless maternal soup, thickening like a plot, yields form, consciousness, and differentiation. The "finger" is admonitory, mocking, and wicked all at once. As with all Kumin's representations of offspring, the newborn does and does not belong to its source. Is earth here a phallic mom? If so, it is but to amuse and not to frighten. Like many another irrational fantasy, facing it dispels the fear.

III.

"My job is metaphor."
—"Lines Written in the Library of Congress"

Disinclined to the egoistic posturing we expect of the artist, Kumin has published few poems about Art. One of those few, "*Ars Poetica:* A Found Poem" in *Looking for Luck,* does not mention poetry but describes the training of a foal:

> I'd go in on my hands
> and knees and crawl over to him so that
> I wouldn't appear so threatening. It took
> six or eight months before I could simply walk in
> and sit with him, but I needed that kind of trust.
>
> I kept him on a long rein to encourage him
> to stretch out his neck and back. I danced with him
> over ten or fifteen acres of fields with a lot
> of flowing from one transition to another.

By implication, the poem is itself a wild creature whom loving patience makes orderly without loss of spirit and energy. As one need not "break" a horse to tame him—and the new methods are apparently making headway even among cowboys—so one can get a poem to cooperate and show its best stuff, by putting it on a long lead (not the same as no lead at all). It is an interesting view of poetry that I haven't seen elsewhere. Similarly lacking in pretension are "Marianne, My Mother, and Me" and "A Brief History of Passion," in which the poet's attachment to artists like Marianne Moore, Katherine Mansfield and Middleton

Murray, D. H. Lawrence and Frieda, Rilke and his mistress, is paired with the attachment to her unexceptional parents—especially the mother who gave up the piano for bourgeois family life. It is as if the poet refuses, against the rules, to honor art above family.

Having written this last sentence, I catch myself. What are these rules, who makes them, and who profits by them? Why should we continue to support the assumption of art's transcendant superiority to our biological affiliations? If what family means is permanent, lifelong, inescapable entanglement in our most ancient and intractable emotions, it also means an inescapable simultaneity of presence and absence, likeness and difference. The fact is, it requires artistry to convey what family signifies in our lives.

Three characteristics of Kumin's style especially promote its familial content. One is a line that moves inconspicuously between three and five feet, rhyming some portion of the time, somewhere between heavy and light. Supporting this is the voice's slightly jocular, conversational tone, a few shades more informal than Frost's. It would be difficult to play dominance games using this voice, and part of Kumin's intention is to dismantle the old, hierarchical models of family, as well as the old, hieratic model of the poet. Most important is the device of the metaphor, especially as it attaches to her otherwise literalizing bent.

A number of postmodern critics have suggested that metaphor is dead. Like the death of the author, the death of "the unified subject," the death of the novel, the death of the lyric (and so on), metaphor's supposed demise speaks to a conviction that the shared literary culture of the past is irretrievably oppressive and that, unless one ruptures its habitual forms, one is invariably trapped. "Language" poets operating on that assumption seem to replace metaphor with metonymy as a means of leveling, as it were, the verbal playing field. Making sure that no term swallows another or blurs another's integrity is a sort of linguistic enforcement of democracy. One word one vote. An unlimited potential set of words, none superior to another (and no subordinate clauses either), is one mark of avant-garde poetics today. Suspicion of metaphor's power to "distort" rational discourse has been a recurrent feature of rationalist philosophies from Bacon and Locke to Wittgenstein, but only recently have poets themselves rejected the defining feature of poetic language.

Such cleaning up of slates could make sense if metaphors were always binary objects composed of clear-cut tenors and vehicles, or if metaphors were always ornamental. They are not—and it seems to me that a poetics that denies metaphor must also deny (and commonly does) the facts of relationship. Aristotle argues in the *Poetics* (1458b) that "the greatest thing by far is to be a master of metaphor. It is the one thing that cannot be learnt from others; and it is also a sign of genius, since a good metaphor implies an intuitive perception of the similarity in dissimilars." A literature that hopes to discourage such perception would disparage metaphor as well.

Kumin's profusely metaphoric style is her primary means of conveying relation, and the ambiguity of relation. Desire is the topic here. In her tribal poems, an ethos of combined sameness/difference, attachment/release, governs personal relationships. The same principles govern her treatment of nature; that is, she represents human beings (chiefly herself) as both alike and different from, attached to and detached from, the richly depicted world of animals and plants. In each specific case life is cyclic, necessarily loved, necessarily lost. Metaphor tacitly underlines this sense of human connection and separation—what Kumin in a tribute to a long marriage calls "our working distance." As a figure of speech, metaphor (Gr. *carry across*) depends precisely on the assertion of likeness in difference. Further, the implication of identity in metaphor, which we as readers must simultaneously accept and reject if any metaphor is to "work," is a figure of desire and of the recognition that desire both succeeds and fails. We (the poet, the readers) want a sense of connection to one another and the world. Metaphor helps us understand that we can and cannot have it. Metaphor bridges gaps of categorical difference while drawing our attention to them. What it carries is a density of information, along with pleasure and pain—pleasure, I would say, overriding pain.

The reader of this essay may look back over its quotations,

or look anywhere in Kumin's poetry, to observe metaphor's multiple functions. For a final example, consider these lines about horses from the opening poem in *Looking for Luck,* "Credo":

> I trust them to run from me, necks arched in a full
> swan's S, tails cocked up over their backs
> like plumes on a Cavalier's hat. I trust them
> to gallop back, skid to a stop, their nostrils
>
> level with my mouth, asking for my human breath
> that they may taste its intent, taste the smell of it.

Without the association of the horses' beauty with nobility and artifice, without the linking of involuntary physicality (breath, taste, smell) with the "higher" faculty of intention, without the quiet assumption that horses can "ask" with their nostrils as normally as we do with our voices, we would have less information and less of a poem. Certainly we would have less pleasure.

Kumin at the end of "Credo" says she believes in herself as the animals' sanctuary and the earth as hers. A sanct-uary is a safe but also an archaically and metaphorically holy location. Etymology here links with an only partially ironic title. The poet's credo, overtly having to do with the connections between humans and animals, covertly is a belief in trope. Secular though she is, Kumin can let metaphor express the belief, which is both true and false, that things are on earth as they are in heaven.

NOTES

1. Maxine Kumin, *Our Ground Time Here Will Be Brief: New and Selected Poems* (New York: Penguin Books, 1982), 3. Other volumes referred to in this essay are *The Long Approach,* 1985; *Nurture,* 1989; and *Looking for Luck,* 1992.

2. Margaret Homans, *Women Writers and Poetic Identity* (Princeton: Princeton University Press, 1980). Homans's *Bearing the Word: Language and Female Experience in Nineteenth-Century Women's Writing* (Chicago and London: University of Chicago Press, 1986) proposes a

tradition of literary language that depends on the repression of the mother and concentrates on Victorian women novelists' response to the dilemma of being defined by the very literature they wish to enter, as "either a speaker or a mother but not both" (38).

3. John Dryden, *Works*, vol. 14 (London: James Ballantyne, 1808), 20.

4. Henry David Thoreau, *Walden* (Princeton: Princeton University Press, 1989), 137–38, 218, 221.

5. For a longer discussion of paradigms in nature poetry, see *Stealing the Language*, 114–19.

6. Wallace Stevens, *Collected Poems* (New York: Vintage, 1990), 507.

7. Gary Snyder, *Turtle Island* (New York: New Directions, 1975), 102, 107.

8. Sandra Gilbert and Susan Gubar, in *The Madwoman in the Attic: The Woman Writer and the Nineteenth-Century Literary Imagination* (New Haven and London: Yale University Press, 1979), 29–34, comment on this recurrent figure in men's writing as one that projects onto women man's "horror of his own carnal contingence," in Simone de Beauvoir's words, and illustrates "infantile dread of maternal autonomy." A nice example is Swift's personification of "Criticism" in *The Battle of the Books* (cited by Gilbert and Gubar, *Madwoman*, 33):

> Her Eyes turned inward, as if she lookt only upon Herself; Her diet was the overflowing of her own Gall; Her Spleen was so large, as to stand prominent like a Dug of the first Rate, nor wanted Excrescencies in forms of Teats, at which a crew of ugly Monsters were greedily sucking; and what is wonderful to conceive, the bulk of spleen increased faster than the Sucking could diminish it.

Kin and Kin

The Poetry of Lucille Clifton

Yes, the work must be political. It must have that as its
thrust. That's a pejorative term in critical circles now: if a
work of art has any political influence in it, somehow it's
tainted. My feeling is just the opposite. . . . It seems to me
that the best art is political and you ought to make it
unquestionably political and irrevocably beautiful at the
same time.
—Toni Morrison, "Rootedness: The Ancestor as
Foundation"

> O for God's sake
> they are connected
> underneath
> —Muriel Rukeyser, "Islands"

From the strong comes forth sweetness. Or perhaps it is the
other way around; perhaps sweetness emanates strength. Or,
as I begin to suspect in tracking Lucille Clifton's dense and
vivid mythmaking, her strength and sweetness derive from a
further source, of which she is an extraordinarily efficient
conduit. I would like, in this essay, to show how spiritually
complicated an apparently "easy" poet can be—and how a
gentle voice can be both revolutionary and revelatory.

I. Adam and His Mother

Lucille Clifton's writing is deceptively simple. The poems are
short, unrhymed, the lines typically between four and two

From *American Poetry Review* (1993). Reprinted in *Literary Influence and
African-American Writers,* ed. Tracy Mishkin (New York: Garland, 1995).

beats. The sentences are usually declarative and direct, the punctuation light, the diction a smooth mix of standard English with varying styles and degrees of black vernacular. Almost nothing (including "i" and beginnings of sentences) is capitalized. Some poems have titles, others do not, a fact that may disconcert the reader and is probably intended to. Marilyn Hacker has written that Clifton's poems remind her, in grace and deftness, of Japanese ink drawings. They remind me of a drum held in a woman's lap. The woman sits on a plain wooden chair or on the earth. A community surrounds her. She slaps the drum with her bare hands. "Oh children," this drummer says in the title poem of Clifton's first book, "think about the good times."

The work of a minimalist artist like Clifton makes empty space resonate. Silence in such art is not mere absence of noise but locates us as it were on a cosmic stage. We are meant to understand the unsaid, to take our humble places with a sense of balance and belonging instead of the anxiety and alienation promoted by more conspicuously sublime and ambitious artistries. Omissions, as Marianne Moore remarks in another context, are not accidents. Whatever the content of a particular piece, we should experience the craftsmanship of the minimalist as a set of unerring gestures governed by a constraining and shaping discipline, so habitual it seems effortless. While the white space in art of this kind stands for the largeness of space and time in which we human creatures find ourselves, the figured space stands for thick experience—experience that has been philosophically contemplated for an extended period. The artist, having patiently learned something quite exact about the dynamics of reality, offers it in concentrated form.

A byproduct of concentration may be humor, the sacred levity associated with adepts in numerous traditions of religious art. Think of the Zen image of the laughing monk; John Cage's playfulness; the jokes of the thirteenth-century Sufi poet Rumi or those in the Chasidic stories told by Martin Buber; the trickster pranks of Coyote in Native American folktales, or Monkey King leaping to the end of the universe and peeing on the Buddha's little finger in a Chinese tale; remember the boyishly erotic mischief of the young Krishna. Then think of how Clifton fuses high comedy and high seriousness when she describes the poetic vocation, a topic most poets approach with a solemnity proportional to their/our insecurity. Clifton's "admonitions," the last poem in *good times,* ends:

> children
> when they ask you
> why is your mama so funny
> say
> she is a poet
> she don't have no sense[1]

Another early poem about her vocation is "prayer," which asks an unnamed listener to "lighten up," wonders why his hand is so heavy on "just poor / me," and receives a response that makes this poem cunningly parallel John Milton's complaint of blindness:

> answer
>
> this is the stuff
> i made the heroes out of
> all the saints
> and prophets and things
> had to come by
> this

Has Clifton read Milton's sonnet, which questions how God can exact the "day-labor" of poetry from a blind man, and ends in the famous "They also serve who only stand and wait"? Whether she has or not, what impresses me (and makes me laugh) is the identical structure of these two poems in which the poet interrogates God's fairness and gets fairly answered—and the marvelous freshness of Clinton's version. It thrills me as an American that this sacred conversation, this *de profundis,* can occur in the vernacular American language. I enjoy the down-home familiarity between Clifton and her God; I applaud a woman lining herself up with the heroes and prophets; and I feel, as well, for her struggle—which is not Milton's blindness, or Gerard Manley Hopkins's conviction of sin, but an American black woman's struggle, which I can guess at. In a much later piece, "the making of poems," humility and comic afflatus again meet:

> the reason why i do it
> though i fail and fail
> in the giving of true names
> is i am adam and his mother
> and these failures are my job.

What does it mean when a woman calls herself "adam and his mother"? The mother could be Eve, or a nameless pre-monotheistic goddess, or just any mother doing her homely work—and that conflation of myth and modernity is part of the joke. Making the poet double gendered is another part.[2] "True names" registers the archaic notion that language is not arbitrary, that poetry names true essences of things—while the poet's failure, it seems to me, conflates individual inadequacy with the imperfect meshing of signifiers and signified in a nonmythic world. How *could* "adam and his mother" find language for the way we live in the twentieth century? Still, they have to try. As with the simple double gesture of "this" to stand for the hardship God inflicts on saints and prophets, the idea of the poet's work as an impossible yet sacred task is effectively rendered in the plainest of language—right down to calling it not a task but a job. "The making of poems" demystifies poetic labor and dignifies maternal and manly labor. What these poems tell us is that high and low things can meet, along with the union of the holy and the comic, if one knows enough about both.

II. Only Connect

Let me talk a little more about meetings and mergings in Clifton, how they bely the poetry's apparent simplicity, and how they feed its spirituality. Born in upper New York State in 1936, Lucille Clifton was the daughter of Sam Clifton, a steelworker, and Thelma Louise, who died at age forty-four. She was the great-granddaughter of Caroline Sale, a Virginia midwife who remembered Africa, the slave ship, and walking from New Orleans to Virginia at the age of eight. She attended Howard University and Fredonia State Teachers' College, met and was influenced by Leroi Jones, Ishmael Reed, and Gwendolyn Brooks. Reed showed some of her poems to Langston Hughes, who published them in an anthology. Robert Hayden sent some to Carolyn Kizer, who sent them to the 1969 YM-WHA Discovery contest, which Clifton won. Her first book of poems was selected by the *New York Times* as one of the ten best books of that same year.

Clifton began writing during the explosive Black Arts movement of the late 1960s and early 1970s, and her early subjects include the memory of slavery, the facts of poverty, urban riots. She mourns assassinated black leaders and praises live ones, tells family stories, records her womanly conversion from bleaching cream and "whiteful ways" to the love of blackness. Black anger and black pride stand at the core of her work. Her family memoir, *Generations,* begins with an epigraph from the Book of Job: "Lo, mine eye hath seen all this, mine ear hath heard and understood it. What ye know, the same do I know also; I am not inferior unto you." The second epigraph, which forms a powerful refrain both in the memoir and in Clifton's poems, quotes "Mammy Ca'line": "Get what you want, you from Dahomey women."

The black inheritance joins others. Walt Whitman's transcendental expansiveness and Emily Dickinson's verbal compression feel uniquely wedded in Clifton. Epigraphs from Whitman mark the sections of *Generations,* and the elliptical Emily might well consider the intensely playful Lucille one of her daughters. Audrey McCluskey notices her Dickinsonian "simultaneous acknowledgment of pain and possibility";[3] I notice the ghost of Emily, who felt the size of her small life swelling like horizons in her breast and "sneered—softly— 'small!' " But unlike either Whitman or Dickinson, Clifton represents herself as implicated in the life of a community, not as observer but as participant. An early instance of her communality would be Clifton's much-anthologized "miss rosie":

when i watch you
wrapped up like garbage
sitting, surrounded by the smell
of too old potato peels
or
when i watch you
in your old man's shoes
with the little toe cut out
sitting, waiting for your mind
like next week's grocery
i say
when i watch you
you wet brown bag of a woman
who used to be the best looking gal in georgia
used to be called the Georgia Rose
i stand up
through your destruction
i stand up

Structurally, this poem resembles a Shakespeare sonnet. The thrice repeated "when i watch you" works in fact like sonnet 64's triple "When I have seen . . ." to produce, section by section, a crescendo of urgency. The verb "watch," like "have seen," implies a sustained attentiveness. Unlike Shakespeare's verb, it also implies intimacy: it tells us that the speaker and the object of her gaze are neighbors. The object of the gaze, the wasted woman, woman-as-garbage, is like the "ruin" of Shakespeare's sonnet, which makes him "ruminate." Beauty decays. Only what time destroys for Shakespeare is for Clifton destroyed by time and poverty joined.

Clifton's closing triplet, like a Shakespearean couplet, throws the poem into another gear. We move abruptly from sitting to standing. You to me. Destruction to survival. Clifton's whiplash has a tightness like Shakespeare's paradoxical sonnet endings: "To love that well which thou must leave ere long." "This thought is as a death, which cannot choose / But weep to have that which it fears to lose." But can we define Clifton's tone? Grief, shame, and compassion govern this poem, we might say, and resolution governs its close. Yet the poem is cruel as well, and I do not think it is simply a matter of facing, confronting, the cruelty of age and poverty. The speaker keeps her distance in the poem. She watches, doesn't touch. Neither is it a protest poem. What of the pivotal preposition "through?" Difficult to pin down, it can mean "despite." Though you fail, I endure. Or it can imply duration or submission. I endure your destruction as if it were a storm pelting me. The gesture signals homage, a salute, almost a military standing at attention. I stand up for you, for your rights, in your honor. Yet "through" can also mean "because of." Your destruction precipitates or causes my survival, my will to survive. I do this for (or instead of) you. I do it because you don't, I triumph because you fail, and even in some sense thanks to your failure.

The reader of "miss rosie" need not be aware of the poem's technical subtlety or its emotional and moral ambiguity; in fact, the subtlety and ambiguity speak precisely to what we habitually repress from consciousness. At the obvious level of content the poem makes us look at what we might prefer not to see: the condition of poverty and hopelessness. At another level it lets us see ourselves—and the awful complexity of our connection to others.

Forster's "Only connect" could be Clifton's motto. Other poets' juvenilia may elaborate the postures of a solitary or romantically alienated self, but Clifton is already maternal, daughterly, a voice at once personal and collective, rooted and relational. The "good times" of her first title poem describe an evening when the family is drunk and dancing in the kitchen because the rent is paid, the lights back on, and an uncle has hit the numbers. The poem urges "oh children / think about the good times" in a voice that could be either rejoicing or begging, and that invites us to the party yet asks us to recognize how that party is circled by pain. An early ecological poem, "generations," begins by invoking the responsibilities of "people who are going to be / in a few years / bottoms of trees," and ends by warning that "the generations of rice / of coal / of grasshoppers // by their invisibility / denounce us." In her kitchen cutting greens, Clifton observes, "i hold their bodies in obscene embrace . . . and the kitchen twists dark on its spine / and i taste in my natural appetite / the bond of live things everywhere."

Her family poems brim with linkages. Poems to and about her mother proliferate and spin through yearning, rue, rivalry, and passionate identification. Her father is adored, pitied, rebuked. Her daughters are "my girls / my almost me" and then "my dearest girls / my girls / my more than me." Or, in a rondeau of relation, "lucy is the ocean / extended by / her girls / are the river / fed by / lucy / is the sun / reflected through / her girls." She addresses her black heroines Harriet Tubman, Sojourner Truth, and her own grandmother, with the refrain "if i be you." In sum, she assumes connection where the dualisms of our culture assume separation— between self and other, humans and nature, male and female, public and private life, pleasure and pain—and what emanates from her mixings, like the wave of energy released when atoms fuse, is something like joy. This is true even when, or especially when, the experience that feeds the poems is of "blood and breaking."

The other side of Clifton's impulse to connect is the gnostic impulse to look inward. In the early work the most obvious form this impulse takes is her brooding on memory and the connection to ancestry and to an Africa that "all of my bones remember." Less conspicuously, she contemplates mental process itself, wondering what kinds of knowledge—material and spiritual, external and internal—may be available to us, what the difference is between appearance and reality. Her first poem about her mother's early death expresses puzzlement as much as pain:

> seemed like what she touched was hers
> seemed like what touched her couldn't hold,
> she got us almost through the high grass
> then seemed like she turned around and ran
> right back in
> right back on in

Her first poem about her father, describing his work, asks

> what do my daddy's fingers
> know about grace?
> what do the couplers know
> about being locked together?

A poem about an abortion asks

> what did i know about waters rushing back
> what did i know about drowning
> or being drowned

The implication is that truth is always somewhere deeper than
words or even actions. In sex a husband "fills / his wife with
children and / with things she never knew." Knowledge is also
"the life thing in us . . . call it craziness . . . call it whatever you
have to / call it anything." The female body is her primary
teacher: "i entered the earth in / a woman jar . . . and it has
made me / wise." The name her mother gave her, Lucille,
means "light," and the poet views her own birth as a symbol of
light breaking. Clifton celebrates the six fingers she had on
each hand at birth, her nappy hair and her free hips, her body
like a city, her tasty and electric sexuality. And again and again
she uses the key figure of "turning" to express her need for
inner life:

> turning out of the
> white cage, turning out of the
> lady cage
> turning at last
> on a stem like a black fruit
>
> (143)

> if in the middle of my life
> i am turning the final turn
> into the shining dark
>
> (159)

> see the sensational
> two-headed woman
> one face turned outward
> one face
> swiveling slowly in

For what the poet discovers within is a woman's epistemology, the radiant life of the spirit.

III. Illuminated Night

The source of Clifton's spiritual strength is black. It is also what she calls, punning on her own name, "the light." It comes, as she has her John the Baptist say in the "some jesus" poems, "in blackness like a star."

"Some jesus," the first of Clifton's revisionist religious sequences, begins like this:

> adam and eve
>
> the names
> of the things
> bloom in my mouth
>
> my body opens
> into brothers

You have to read that twice before you realize how simply and stunningly androgynous a poem it is—how lucidly it represents what Robert Hass, speaking of Rilke, calls "the pull inward, the erotic pull of the other we sense buried in the self," but represents it as achieved, not merely desired. The poet distinguishes male and female selves, voices, roles, but doesn't separate them from each other or from herself: she is both, they are both she. Casually proceeding then to inhabit the male personae of Cain, Moses, Solomon, Job, Daniel, and Jonah, Clifton's voice in the New Testament section of this sequence slides into the voice of a John who could be in Galilee or Philadelphia praising a savior—

> he be calling the people brother
> even in the prison
> even in the jail;

then into the voice of a Mary whose annunciation is erotic, a kiss "as soft as cotton / over my breasts / all shiny bright," a disciple who doesn't mind "laughing like god's fool / behind this jesus"; a Lazarus whose raising is also a promise of revolution,

> whoever say
> dust must be dust
> don't see the trees
> smell rain
> remember africa;

a Jesus on "good friday" who says "i rise up above myself / like a fish flying / men will be gods / if they want it"; and a final "spring song" celebrating the green rebirth of "delicious jesus." Gloria Ashaka Hull has observed that Clifton feminizes, Africanizes, eroticizes, and makes mystical the biblical stories she uses. I would add that she is recovering and restoring forms of myth and worship that white tradition has all but erased,[4] and that her intimacy or fusion with biblical personas fulfills on the stage of the inner life what her "if i be you" does with the kin of her outer life.

As her career proceeds, Clifton's spirituality grows bolder and more syncretic. In "to a dark moses" of Clifton's third book, *an ordinary woman,*

> you are the one
> i am lit for.
> come with your rod
> that twists
> and is a serpent.
> i am the bush.
> i am burning.
> i am not consumed.

If we take this poem literally, and why should we not, God is a black woman who is also Lucille Clifton. In the sequence of Kali poems it is indeed "a woman god and terrible / with her skulls and breasts" who pushes past the poet's fear and resistance, enters her bones, and forces her to say, "i know i am your sister." Admitting the goddess of death as a portion of herself—of ourselves—is Clifton's most radical move in *an ordinary woman.* The poet's next book, *two-headed woman,* includes a sequence of eight poems voicing the life of Mary in a dialect that thickens toward Caribbean, implies a braiding of Christianity and Rastafarianism, and emphatically fuses eroticism and spirituality, exaltation and fear, with her increasingly characteristic light imagery:

> joseph, i cannot still these limbs,
> i hands keep moving toward i breasts,
> so many stars. so bright.
> joseph, is wind burning from east
> joseph, i shine, oh joseph,   oh
> illuminated night.

Clifton also lets us feel the human pain of this "chosen" woman whose womb blossoms then dies. Mary's mother Anna wants to "fight this thing." Mary in her last poem has become a weary "old creature" wondering, "could i have walk away when voices / singing in my sleep," prophetically worrying about another girl whom a star might choose.

At about this time Clifton's spirituality unmoors itself from scripture. "Breaklight" testifies to a visionary synesthesia of inner light and language: "light keeps on breaking" with the spirit voices of "other nations," trees, water, which the poet mysteriously understands—and then the light reveals itself as the hesitant fears of the poet's dead mother. Uncannily parallel to Dylan Thomas's "Light breaks where no sun shines," the poem opens itself to a kind of holy breaking and entering. That process, writ large and terrifying, becomes the theme of "the light that came to lucille clifton," the final sequence in *two-headed woman*. These excruciating poems delineate the poet's experiences of incandescent light infused with soft voices that at first make her fear madness. Only gradually does she identify the voices of light as wingless angels, as parents, as the dead: "in populated air / our ancestors continue . . . i have heard / their shimmering voices / singing."

ఇ▲

Numerous writers have testified to the force of religion in African-American writing. "Mystical longings, a desire to transcend empirical boundaries and material limitations are . . .

the entrancing essence of Afro-America," writes Houston Baker. Derek Walcott notes, "I have never separated the writing of poetry from prayer." Toni Morrison, Alice Walker, Toni Cade Bambara, Paule Marshall, and Audre Lorde are a few of the black writers who make visionary sutures of material and spiritual existence. Yet no other writer approaches Clifton's capacity to carry us from fragmentation to wholeness. Thus in the poem elliptically entitled "I. at creation," in her 1987 volume *Next,* when she begins with "i and my body," we might think of the traditional duality of body and soul, but Clifton draws them coupled instead of adversarial:

> and i and my body rise
> with the dusky beasts
> with eve and her brother
> to gasp in
> the unsubstantial air
> and evenly begin the long
> slide out of paradise.
> all life is life.
> all clay is kin and kin.

The moment of "creation" here is both past and continual; it is inseparable from and contiguous with a departure from (not "loss" of) paradise; it perhaps includes the creation of the poem; it is the trauma and triumph of birth, and all creatures share it. At the same time there are the muted ironies, the understanding that a black woman is to be identified with "dusky beasts," but then again with "eve and her brother," and the tacit argument for kinship made by the assonance of "beasts," "eve," "evenly." The assonance of "i" and "rise" at the poem's opening returns with the "slide" from "paradise" and is reinforced in the next line, which then yields to the alliteration of the final line, as if an argument were being closed. Isn't it closed? Isn't it obvious? The poem's physicality is one with its logic. As readers, we perceive ourselves rising amid a multitude of others, gasping like newborns, sliding involuntarily, and arriving at what feels like certain knowledge. The experience of creation, coterminous with the shedding of safety, is the one touch of nature that unifies the world—and the poet makes it seem the most natural thing in the world.

IV. The Ways of Death

Having read and taught Lucille Clifton for years, I need to suggest the myriad ways she delights me, invites me, strengthens and supports me as artist, woman, earthy visionary. I need also to talk about the shadow that is inseparable from the pleasure I take in Clifton's work. That shadow is, of course, race.

You can walk in another's shoes, the saying goes, but you cannot walk in his skin. So I can identify with Clifton's voice, presence, and power despite my whiteness and her blackness. The poems make me do that. By being strong and sweet, the poems strengthen and sweeten me. And of course I've seen the same thing happen to others—seen, for example, a whole classroom of white undergraduates break into smiles when I've read "Homage to My Hair" and "Homage to My Hips," not because these girls had nappy hair or big hips themselves but because Clifton's self-affirmation was contagious. "These hips are big hips / these hips are mighty hips / these hips have never been enslaved" made affirmation feel possible, made everywoman feel momentarily capable of overcoming our commerce-fueled and misogyny-driven disapproval of our own bodies.

Black writers commonly appeal in this way to white readers: they pull us out of ourselves into the condition of the Other, while their power and courage—as writers, as humans—empower and encourage us. In a sense, this is the function of all strong imaginative writing, in any language. It carries across boundaries as nothing else can do. Yet we delude ourselves if we think that writing in fact (as well as fancy) eliminates difference. I cannot inhabit Clifton's skin. I cannot in fact share her ancestors or her experience as a black woman in America. The pride and anger that vitalize her work can only vicariously, never actually, be mine. And whether I wish it or not—and I don't, and have resisted the knowledge, trying to remain unaware of what Clifton was finally showing me against my will—the pride excludes, and the anger targets, my whiteness. "Kin and kin" notwithstanding, the poems draw a circle in the sand. I stand hurt, outside.

For the absence of militant rhetoric from Clifton's poetry doesn't mean absence of bitterness. I think of Blake's "Chimney-Sweep" in *Songs of Experience,* an indictment of the complacent London rich: "Because I am happy and dance and sing / They think they have done me no injury." A black person lacking a sense of injury in this country is either a very small child, or a fool, or a traitor. What must it feel like to live in a pool of hatred? To know that you are despised (as well as unconsciously envied) by the majority of your fellow citizens? To have seen your leaders and heroes assassinated, your schoolchildren spat on, your churches bombed? To know that your boys and men can be killed—are killed—by white boys and men who typically go unpunished? That your women are just brown sugar? How does it feel to live in a nation whose laws scarcely intend to protect your life, your liberty, or your pursuit of happiness?

Part of what separates white from black America, I suspect, is that if whites actually tried to imagine being black, we'd go mad with pain and rage. To be privileged is to be fragile. If I were a young black man, it seems to me entirely likely that I would be among the killers or the killed. If I were the mother of a young black man, it seems to me the daily terror and despair would strangle me. Yet I can no more *enter* that despair than I can imagine myself a Jew *in* the Holocaust rather than saved from it. Clifton, on the other hand, defines herself without raising her voice:

> i got a long memory
> and i come from a line
> of black and going on women
> who got used to making it through murdered sons

She defines, in a tone of patient explanation, what young black males feel:

they act like they don't love their country
no
what it is
is they found out
their country don't love them.

Clifton's stance toward white culture varies from the wry mockery of the first poem in *good times,* with its double sneer at repression and euphemism:

in the inner city
or
like we call it
home
we think a lot about uptown
and the silent nights
and the houses straight as dead men
and the pastel lights

to the scornful pity of "after kent state," written after National Guardsmen shot four students demonstrating against the invasion of Cambodia during the Vietnam War:

only to keep
his little fear
he kills his cities
and his trees
even his children   oh
people
white ways are
the ways of death

to a bit of acerbic mythmaking:

the once and future dead
who learn they will be white men
weep for their history. we call it
rain.

The title poem of *good news about the earth* predicts the destruction of white men by mountains and waters, enabling their bodies to join those of Native Americans broken on the Trail of Tears, slaves melted into the ocean floor of Middle Passage. The celebratory and affirmative Clifton possesses this calm judge at her core, just as the Christian Clifton contains a black and ruthless Hindu goddess.

In *next* (1987), a series of poems on South Africa, and another on the death of Crazy Horse, join poems about Gettysburg, Buchenwald, Nagasaki, Jonestown, and the Shatila massacre in Lebanon, indicting "the extraordinary evil / in ordinary men." These in turn join a set of anguished poems describing a young girl's struggle with leukemia, some luminously elegiac poems about the death of her husband, Fred, some communings with her dead mother, a rueful sequence about doing poetry readings "in white america," the "shapeshifter poems" on incest, the "california lessons" on race and karma. Though a book filled with grief and grievances, it makes room for the pleasure of grandchildren; it also makes room for a meditation on the poet's own capacity for cruelty— a poem about killing cockroaches. In one mischievous poem, "my dream about being white," the poet imagines herself with "no lips, no behind, hey" wearing white history:

> but there's no future
> in those clothes
> so i take them off and
> wake up
> dancing.

Now, to a poem like this, how can I respond but doubly? Lucid, funny, self-loving poem, I think. "If I be you," I want to say to its author, "let me remember to respect my own dreams." Yet to be mocked for my no lips and no backside grieves me; to be assured that my race has no future grieves me; I don't believe it, any more than I believe that white people's ways are "ways of death" rather than abuses of power, which black people would/will/do abuse too when they have equal opportunity. Hey, honey, I want to respond; I don't demonize you, so don't you demonize me.

Yet there is more; and as a white woman it behooves me to

think further. What is the "little fear" of which Clifton speaks, the fear that generates "the ways of death" in American foreign policy, domestic policy, economic policy—and how complicit am I in it? It could be the fear of losing control. It could be the fear of empathizing with the Other, the fear of suffering. Three decades ago James Baldwin, in *The Fire Next Time*, claimed that white Americans do not face "reality—the fact that life is tragic . . . but people who cannot suffer can never grow up."[5] I find that argument rather persuasive.

One wants to feel loved back by what one loves. It doesn't necessarily happen. Why should it? It won't kill me, comfortable as I otherwise am, to experience now and again the kind of hurt a black person feels every day. Race forms one of the two most basic divisions among human beings—gender is the other—that have stood since history began as excuses for hatred, violence, exploitation. All societies, all peoples, are racist. That victims as well as oppressors can be racist is hardly news. No solution in sight, the best we can do is listen to one another, and the privileged need to listen harder.

Clifton has addressed the problem of speaking across race explicitly. The sequence "in white america" records a black poet's loneliness and alienation in a town where she's been invited to read—a town where a century ago the Native American longhouses and crops were burned "by not these people here," and dark women scrubbed the floor of the church where no dark woman could rise to worship. Her lady tour guide means well:

> "this was a female school,
> my mother's mother graduated
> second in her class.
> they were taught embroidery,
> and chenille and filigree,
> ladies' learning. yes,
> we have a liberal history here."
> smiling she pats my darky hand.

Those are not lines I can read without wincing—for the poet's sake and for my own. Am I that innocent and ignorant "she"?

Do I too condescend, smilingly appropriate, complacently pat the darky hands of the black writers I think I'm admiring and loving? At the reading the poet looks at the audience, which is "none of my faces," and does the best she can: "the human hair between us / stretches but does not break." For the time being, that may be the best anyone can expect.

V. Lucifer/Lucille

Quilting: Poems 1987–1990, Clifton's boldest book, continues her meditations on history, loss, tragedy. Her affirmation of the body continues in two glorious poems on menstruation, followed by the hilarious "wishes for sons," which fantasizes for them cramps, the last tampon, one week early, one week late, hot flashes and clots, and gynecologists resembling themselves.

But the most important work in this volume is the ten-poem "Tree of Life" sequence, a lyric reimagining of the role of Lucifer in Eden. "How art thou fallen from heaven, oh Lucifer, son of the morning," cries Isaiah 14:12. Clifton's version of the myth makes Lucifer (Lat. *light-bringer*) at once light, lightning, and snake, servant of God, illuminator of mankind.[6] As in the "some jesus" poems, the poet speaks through plural voices that seem to inhabit her. Hers is the voice of the mystified angels describing Lucifer's creation and fall in the first three poems, then woman's sensuous voice in "eve's version" and man's sensually and intellectually desperate one in "adam thinking." Most fascinatingly, her voice is also Lucifer's.

Clifton's possession of and by the spirit of Lucifer, whose name echoes hers, and who is "six-fingered" like her, is an identification with masculine creativity. When the rather neoplatonic seraphim ponder "was it the woman / enticed you to leave us," Lucifer confirms and globalizes his sexuality:

> bearer of lightning
> and of lust
>
> thrust between the
> legs of the earth
> into this garden

> phallus and father
> doing holy work
>
> oh sweet delight
> oh eden

The trajectory of "Tree of Life" is from heaven to earth, creation to final day, ignorance to knowledge. Part of its charm is its teasing allusiveness, its indeterminacies and uncertainties. When the "shine" of Lucifer's birth seems too much for "one small heaven," should we be reminded of the breaking of vessels, which in kabbala is the moment of creation? When Lucifer leaves heaven in shadow,

> and even the
> solitary brother
> has risen from his seat
> of stones   he is holding
> they say   a wooden stick
> and pointing toward
> a garden,

is the brother (never mentioned again) Death, or Christ, or the original black man? Is the stick the Tree of Life, the Cross, or both? The unidentified speaker of "the garden of delight"— sixth poem in the sequence—invokes possible Edens of earth, air, fire, and water "for some," using an alchemical scheme, concluding with the quintessential Eden of the poet:

> and for some
> certain only of the syllables
> it is the element they
> search their lives for
>
> eden
>
> for them
> it is a test

Ambiguities converge here. First, that poets may find Eden only in certain syllables (not all of them), or that syllables are the only things they are certain of. Then, that they spend their lives searching, or that they search *within* their lives. Is Eden, then, internal or external? Do words lead to it, or is it embodied in them? Is the test finding Eden, or living in it?

In the penultimate poem uncertainty moves toward certitude. Eve has whispered her knowledge of names to Adam, and the unidentified voice describes the threesome of "the story thus far." As in Clifton's earlier "creation," the time might be the year zero or the day before yesterday: "so they went out / clay and morning star / following the bright back / of the woman." (I recall, in this vista, Whitman's Adam with his Eve "by my side or back of me . . . or in front, and I following her.") As they pass the gate "into the unborn world," the imagery grows brighter, chaos falls away, "and everywhere seemed light / seemed glorious/seemed very eden." Again the fall is not a fall but a birth, the light of Eros and knowledge still surrounds the protagonists, or *seems* to. The "seemed," though inconspicuous, is crucial. Not until the final poem do incertainties crown themselves assured. In the sequence's last poem "lucifer speaks in his own voice"; the light-bringer snake knows he has done God's will and is

> certain of a
> graceful bed
> and a soft caress
> along my long belly
> at endtime.

But only in the final lines does his voice finally merge with the poet's, as if to summarize her career so far:

> illuminate i could
> and so
> illuminate i did.

That is the simplest possible description of Clifton's work.

NOTES

1. Lucille Clifton, *Good Woman: Poems and a Memoir, 1969–1980* (Brockport, N.Y.: Boa Editions, Ltd., 1987), 51. Unless indicated, all

Clifton quotations are from this volume. Other volumes of her poetry quoted are *Next: New Poems* (Brockport, N.Y.: Boa 1987); *Quilting Poems, 1987–1990* (Brockport, N.Y.: Boa 1991); and *The Book of Light* (Port Townsend, Wash.: Copper Canyon 1993).

2. The great facilitator here, as in so much other work that women poets and third world poets do, is of course the Whitman who was "of the woman as well as the man," not contained between his hat and boots, the Whitman who could joke, "I find I incorporate gneiss"—in other words, the Whitman of unlimited sympathies and a fluid "I." But it is important to remember that Emily Dickinson, too, liked to represent herself as male from time to time and to identify herself with biblical figures of both genders. Her rueful poem about going forth like David against Goliath—"I took my Power in my Hand"—has a tone very like Clifton's.

3. Audrey McCluskey, "Tell the Good News: A View of the Works of Lucille Clifton," in *Black Women Writers,* ed. Mari Evans (New York: Doubleday, 1984), 142.

4. Or maybe not erased at all? Jesus as a version of earlier dying-and-reviving gods may be cultural anthropology to the scholar but living religion to an African American. So may goddesses, priestesses, spirit possession, the sacralization of nature and sexuality, and the collapse of gender polarities during worship. For illumination on the survivals of African religion and ritual in the diaspora, see Robert Thompson, *Flash of the Spirit* (New York: Vintage, 1984), a study of Caribbean voodoo and how it syncretizes gods and rituals from various African cultures; Zora Neale Hurston, *Tell My Horse* (Berkeley: Turtle Island, 1983) and *The Sanctified Church* (Berkeley: Turtle Island, 1981); Louis Mars, *The Crisis of Possession in Voodoo* (Berkeley: Reed, Cannon and Johnson, 1977); and Houston A. Baker Jr., *Workings of the Spirit: The Poetics of Afro-American Women's Writing* (Chicago: University of Chicago Press, 1991). Baker's description of classic African-American spiritual performance, in his chapter on Hurston, applies beautifully to Clifton. See also Karen McCarthy, *Mama Lola: A Vodou Priestess in Brooklyn* (Berkeley: University of California Press, 1991).

5. James Baldwin, *The Fire Next Time* (London: Penguin Books, 1964), 84.

6. Barbara G. Walker, in *The Women's Encyclopedia of Myths and Secrets* (San Francisco: Harper and Row, 1983), traces Lucifer to Canaanite myths in which he represents heavenly masculine fire fertilizing the abyss, notes that he "continued to be linked with both lust and lightning during the Christian era," and claims that Gnostic

Christians down to the fourteenth-century mystic Meister Eckhart interpret him as a bringer of enlightenment, a hero, savior, and revealer of sacred mysteries. I am grateful to Ashaka Hull for noticing Clifton's use of Walker and for many other insights into the poet's use of biblical material.

"Howl" Revisited

The Poet as Jew

I. Ginsberg the Yid

It was the best of times; it was the worst of times. It was 1966. We were in Vietnam but thought in our antiwar innocence that we might be out soon. Medgar Evers and Malcolm X were dead but Robert Kennedy and Martin Luther King were still alive. The Chicago riots, the invasion of Cambodia, the killing of four students at Kent State, hadn't happened yet. Allen Ginsberg was giving a reading at Princeton University with Gary Snyder. In Princeton I lived at that time disguised as a young faculty wife and mother of two. Simultaneously at Rutgers University I went to work disguised as a promising young scholar of late-eighteenth- and early nineteenth-century poetry and prosody. Officially I was a Blakean. My own poetry remained in the closet during the years of my assistant professorship; had my colleagues known of my folly, I would probably not have gotten the job, since most of them considered creative writing the equivalent of basket weaving, an activity for the retarded. Also in the closet were my two daughters in diapers. One did not discuss family in my department, where my senior colleagues were witty and charming men who all looked and behaved as if they had never in their lives laid eyes on a diaper.

I had already heard Allen once, at Rutgers, where he took off the top of my head in the standing room only vault of Voorhees Chapel by introducing as his opening act, of all people, his father Louis Ginsberg. Louis, with considerable

From *American Poetry Review* (July–August 1997).

self-importance, read some of his own poetry—rhymed, re-fined, culturally anonymous lyrics—as if to say this is how it should be done, here's the real thing, now you can listen to my son. Louis' condescension was not a joke, it was real. Equally real was Allen's affectionate graciousness toward his dad. As the daughter of a mother who also wrote rhymed poetry, of the same vintage as Louis's, I was overwhelmed. I couldn't *dream* of doing a reading with my mom. Embarrassing! Impossible! Couldn't dream of achieving the spiritual state that would make such openness possible for me.... But what if . . . ? And indeed, a mere twenty years later, I found myself able to do it, give readings with my mother. Not often, not easily, but with a certain amount of grace that would have been impossible for me without that distant model.

In Princeton Allen read "Please Master," and I was scandalized. But I had a question to ask him and at the post-reading party I fought my way through the crowd of adoring boy undergraduates to ask it. It concerned his voice. That sonorous, sweet, deep, vibrant, patient baritone seemed to emerge from some inexhaustible energy source, manifesting the double sense of *spiritus* as simultaneously breath and spirit. But I had listened to an early recording of "Howl" in which, far from having the long lines express the poet's "natural" breath units as he so often claimed, the voice was high-pitched and short-breathed—entirely *un*equal to the long lines. What about it? Did he really develop the voice to go with the lines, and not the other way around? Yes, he cheerfully agreed, he had written the lines to go with his *potential* voice. And how, I asked—for this was what I wished to learn—did he train his voice to do what it did now? Could I do that? Allen smiled and suggested filling the bathtub and lying in the water face down reciting poems. Then he took another look at me and said: It's not so hard. Just do the breathing exercises you learned in childbirth classes.

The breathing exercises I had learned in childbirth classes. How did this gay guy, who knew nothing about women, know at a glance that the shy chick in front of him had taken childbirth classes? How did he know that pregnancy and childbirth had been, for her, peak spiritual experiences? I wanted to kiss his sandals. I watched him then with the flock of Princeton boys and saw how he listened to each one with the same focused attention, responding to each according to his need. It occurred to me that he didn't just want to sleep with them. He wanted to love them.

ۏ

There is a word in Hebrew for a virtue at the core of Ginsberg's character and his writing, a virtue that has been noticed by infinite numbers of people—*chesed*. It means kindness, or lovingkindness.[1] *Chesed* is one of thirteen attributes of God according to Maimonides (who gets it from Exod. 34.6); it is, in addition, a quality of Torah (a Jew expresses gratitude each day to the God who has given us a Torah of life, and lovingkindness, and righteousness, and compassion, and peace); it is a quality highly regarded among traditional Jewish men, whom Talmud praises as "compassionate sons of compassionate fathers."

In no way could the young Allen Ginsberg have *known* any of this in the secular family in which he grew up, which was not merely secular but adamantly atheist. And yet these ideals would have saturated the air he breathed, for Jewish atheism in its Eastern European sources is fueled by the dream of social justice, which is also a dream of human kindness. In the classic East European Yiddish literature whose shtetl ethos was the mulch from which Louis Ginsberg's socialism and Naomi Ginsberg's communism fed, Irving Howe describes what he calls the value of "sweetness," "the tone of love . . . with which such masters as Sholem Aleichem and Peretz faced the grimmest facts about Jewish life." Howe's further remarks on the fictions of Mendele and Scholem Aleichem, Peretz, Singer, and Jacob Glatstein, might well describe "Howl": "The virtue of powerlessness, the power of helplessness, the company of the dispossessed, the sanctity of the insulted and injured—these, finally are the great themes of Yiddish literature"[2] in which, as well, we find the humor (self-mocking, buffoonish, absurd), the acerbity, the irremediable pain and melancholy a millimeter below the surface, which we find also in Allen Ginsberg.

Sholem Aleichem's village of Kasrilevke and Greenwich Village? Singer's saintly Gimpel the fool and Ginsberg's angel-headed hipsters? Or, still more appallingly/appealingly, a "chosen people"—chosen for persecution, for pogroms, for the chimneys—reincarnated as "the best minds of my generation?" Like the Jews of Europe, Ginsberg's "best minds" suffer for a stubborn adherence to their faith. Yiddishkeit and Ginsberg? A mere generation of partial American assimilation divides them. Ginsberg in "Howl" will record, in veiled fashion, the humiliation and crippling of a population of immigrants to shores that promised hope and produced despair. He will gather the threads dropped by the revolutionary poetry of the 1930s, left dangling in the winter of McCarthyism. He will *schpritz* shamelessly alongside Henny Youngman and Lenny Bruce. Think of his extraordinary language. Ginsberg's beat lexicon, his determination to write a *low* dialect opposed to the literary diction promoted by his one-time mentor Lionel Trilling, may have been supported by William Carlos Williams. But it is also a tribute to his Yiddish-speaking ancestors and the obscure longevity of their gift for juicy emotional tragicomedy.

II. Ginsberg the Prophet

"People have been comparing me to Whitman, and although I love and adore and am a child of Whitman, both of us come from the Bible . . . We are talking about the endless quarrel between the establishment and the prophets, and I hope to be forever on the side of the prophets."

That is not Allen Ginsberg; it is Muriel Rukeyser, a poet a generation earlier, sprung from an assimilated Jewish family of quite another class from Ginsberg's; but one feels it *might* be Allen. Here, I want to argue, is the second area of the poet's Jewishness: if his personal style is an American incarnation of the Yiddish personality, his moral power descends in a direct line from the power of Hebrew prophecy. Certainly "prophet" and "prophetic" are terms that are freely used about his work[3] and that he often uses himself. Describing his 1948 Blake-inspired visions "he realized," Paul Portugés tells us, "that his visionary experiences were not unlike the calling forth of the Hebrew prophets by their Creator" and that his task as a poet would be to recreate "a prophetic illuminative seizure." But the notion of the poet as prophet is a loose one. From the Greek *prophetes,* interpreter or proclaimer, or one who speaks for a deity, the term has been used in the English tradition since the late eighteenth century to denote a variety of sublimities opposed to neoclassic rationality. Jean Wojcik and Raymond-Jean Frontain define a "prophetic" stance in Western art as implying private vision, an insistence on the righteousness of the prophet and the corruption of his society, passionate and hyperbolic language, social radicalism, stylistic obscurity or incoherence, and "obsession, fine or frenzied," as "with every technique of language he can muster, the prophet delivers a message that never arrives." Herbert N. Schneider proposes a definition of the prophet as one who forces people to "look at their culture and see a myth . . . they can no longer believe in, for it is a living lie."[4]

In his 1967 *Paris Review* interview Ginsberg describes the genesis of "Howl": "I thought I wouldn't write a *poem* but just write what I wanted to without fear, let my imagination go, open secrecy, and scribble magic lines from my real mind." Begining Part 1, he found himself composing "a tragic custard-pie comedy of wild phrasing, meaningless images for the beauty of abstract poetry of mind," and got excited and went on, "continuing to prophecy what I really know, despite the drear consciousness of the world."[5] In Ginsberg's 1971 *New York Quarterly* interview with William Packard he remarks of "Howl" that "the poetic precedent for this situation is like Ezekiel and Jeremiah and the Hebrew prophets in the bible who were warning Babylon against its downfall . . . they were talking about the fall of a city like Babylon, or the fall of a tribe, and cursing out the sins of a nation." Now, what is wrong with this picture is that it suggests a view of the Hebrew prophets that charity might call at best sketchy. Jerusalem, not Babylon, for example, is the city warned and mourned by Ezekiel and Jeremiah. The degree to which Ginsberg nonetheless reproduces not merely the King James cadences and rhetoric but the essential contradictions of Hebrew prophecy (as against Christian adaptations) is all the more startling. I want to argue here that the "prophetic" work "Howl" most resembles is the Lamentations of Jeremiah.[6]

Extremity is the groundnote of prophecy. Condemnation and warning dominate pre-exilic prophecy, eschatological promises dominate post-exilic. But where Isaiah and Ezekiel are inspired by and speak for the God of the Covenant, the voice of Lamentations howls in a void: God is terrifyingly present as an agent of destruction yet terrifyingly absent from discourse. Invoked and prayed to out of the depths, he does not reply. But it is precisely the failure of divine response that has produced, as Alan Mintz argues, a literature of catastrophe that itself is an agent of survival:

> Jewish society . . . has had many massive individual catastrophes visited upon it and still survived; and in each case the reconstruction was undertaken in significant measure by the exertions of the Hebrew literary imagination. . . . It is the story of the transcendence of the catastrophe rather than of the catastrophe itself which is compelling.[7]

The City of Jerusalem was sacked, its temple destroyed, in 587 B.C.E. Most of the population sought exile; those who remained suffered famine. If the witness of the Book of Lamentations is to be believed, some of those who remained fed on the bodies of dead children. Emerging from a prophetic paradigm according to which "destruction is . . . a deserved and necessary punishment for sin," which "allows a penitent remnant to survive in a rehabilitated restored relationship to God," Lamentations deviates from the paradigm in that confession of sin in this poem is vastly secondary to "the experience of abandonment and the horror of destruction." The task of the poet is "to find adequate language for the horror." Crucial to Lamentations—and to the genre that will succeed it—is first of all that God, and not a mere human adversary, is the ultimate destroyer, and second that "God remains silent . . . but the sufferer's emergence from soliloquy to prayer enables him at least to recover God as the addressible other"[8] and not merely as a brutal enemy.

&

Between Lamentations and "Howl" the parallels are numerous and uncanny, commencing with the one-word title promising a discourse in the semiotic register of meaningless sound. Outside, or prior to, the Law: the lament. Beyond or before the symbolic register, a howl. A language of vowels. A memory between or among the lines, of the universal inconsolable infant for whom the umbilicus to the Absolute is broken. The infant without boundaries, the I who is Other, or infinite, or zero, witness and victim, betrayed by the word, unable to speak a word. The shriek of the powerless feminized male child.

In both poems the voice is exclamatory, impassioned, hyperbolic, intensely figurative, and virtually impossible to pin down, to locate, to identify. In both, the speaking or shrieking or wailing "I" oscillates between individual and collective identity. In the first chapter of Lamentations the baffled third-person lament—"How doth the city sit solitary, that was full of people! How is she become as a widow!" (1.1) slides without warning, in mid-verse, into first-person: "All her people sigh, they seek bread; they have given their pleasant things for meat to relieve the soul: see, O Lord, and consider; for I am become vile" (1.11). Note that "pleasant things" in this passage is a euphemism for sexual organs; the image is of a starving woman prostituting herself. And again, "Is it nothing to you, all ye that pass by? Behold, and see if there be any sorrow like unto my sorrow which is done unto me, wherewith the Lord hath afflicted me in the day of his fierce anger" (1.12). Is this "I" the defiled and deserted Jerusalem speaking? Or a narrator identifying with her? Impossible to say, and the whole opening chapter refuses to differentiate. Chapter 2 is inhabited by a voice recounting, with horror, the unthinkable hostilities of the Lord against his own people and artifacts: "The Lord was an enemy, he hath swallowed up Israel, he hath swallowed up all her palaces, he hath destroyed his strongholds . . . And he hath violently taken away his tabernacle . . . he hath destroyed his places of the assembly" (2.5–6). But the voice shifts into first person to exclaim, "Mine eyes do fail with tears, my bowels are troubled, my liver is poured out upon the earth, for the destruction of the daughter of my people" (2.11) and then to bewail the impossibility of metaphor or comfort. "What thing shall I liken to thee, O daughter of Jerusalem? What shall I equal to thee, that I may comfort thee . . . For thy breach is great like the sea; who can heal thee?" (2.13). In 3.1 an "I" witnesses distinctly: "I am the man that hath seen affliction"—it is this line which produces Whitman's "I am the man, I suffered, I was there"—and almost immediately *is* afflicted: "My flesh and my skin hath he made old; he hath broken my bones" (3.4). Toward the close of Lamentations 4 and throughout 5 the pronouns shift again, toward a first-person plural, a "we."

In the first moment of "Howl," "I saw the best minds of my generation destroyed by madness, starving hysterical naked, / dragging themselves through the negro streets at dawn looking for an angry fix," and the voice dissolves into what is seen. The "I" releases itself or is released into its surge of empathic madness. In Blakean terms, Ginsberg becomes what he beholds, an anaphoric catalogue of self-destructive souls whose search for the "ancient heavenly connection" that is simultaneously revelation and drug dealer, fails to find the "fix" that would be simultaneously a practical repair and a drugged ecstasy. No further "I" enters the poem until the middle of Part II, where Ginsberg briefly interrupts his invocation/exorcism of the sacrificial deity of industrial capitalist rationality, "Moloch whose name is the Mind," with a spurt of self—"Moloch in whom I sit lonely! Moloch in whom I dream Angels! Crazy in Moloch! Cocksucker in Moloch! Lacklove and manless in Moloch!"—and almost immediately disappears from his own text again. Only in Part III, with the intimate and affectionate address to a friend that parallels the "we" of Lamentations chapter 4, and the refrain "I'm with you in Rockland," does the poem at last imagine a possibility of coherent identity, an "I" in relatively stable relation to a "you." In the "Footnote," personal identity is again transcended; no "I" interrupts the absurd utterance of ecstasy.

The importance of geography in both Lamentations and "Howl" is likewise central and likewise paradoxical and contradictory. In both poems, identity is not only collective but requires rootedness in place. The city, Zion, the daughter of

Zion, Jerusalem, the cities of Judah. Hallucinating Arkansas, poles of Canada and Paterson, Battery to holy Bronx. In both, the connection of place and people has been ruptured—by starvation literal and figurative, by conquest and exile: place does not *sustain* what should be its people, and hence *identity* is impossible.

The rhetoric of both poems relies on sexual figures and on body images, especially images of sexual humiliation and public disgrace. The pain of Jerusalem is also shame: "The adversaries saw her" (1.7). "They have seen her nakedness" (1.8). "Her filthiness is in her skirts" (1.9). "The adversary hath spread out his hand upon all her pleasant things . . . the heathen entered into her sanctuary" (1.10). "Jerusalem is as a menstruous woman" (1.17). The male speaker experiences God as fire in his bones, a net for his feet, a yoke on his neck (1.13–14). In 2.11, "Mine eyes do fail with tears, my bowels are troubled, my liver is poured out upon the earth for the destruction of the daughter of my people." In 2.16, Zion's enemies "hiss and gnash the teeth." In 3.4, "my flesh and skin he hath made old, he hath broken my bones." In 3.16, "he hath broken my teeth with gravel stones." Likewise in Ginsberg Part I, the body is constantly at issue and the issue is commonly exposure, humiliation, deprivation: "starving hysterical naked" comrades "bared their brains to Heaven under the El," "got busted in their pubic beards," "purgatoried their torsos," "broke down crying in white gymnasiums naked," "were dragged off the roof waving genitals and manuscripts," "let themselves be fucked in the ass by saintly motorcyclists, and screamed with joy," "walked all night with their shoes full of blood on the snowbank docks," "cut their wrists three times successively unsuccessfully," and so on. Extremity of spirit is enacted through bodily extremity, the crowning image of which in both poems is cannibalism. In a moment of climactic horror after describing famine in the city, and accusing God of causing it, Lamentations asks, "Shall the women eat their fruit, and children of a span long?" (2.20). At the close of "Howl" Part I, Ginsberg evokes "the absolute heart of the poem of life butchered out of their own bodies good to eat a thousand years."

What Lamentations and "Howl" share most crucially is the anguished and intolerable sense of a divine power that thwarts, punishes, and destroys, that seems absolutely cruel rather than merely indifferent to human suffering, that cannot be appealed to and that remains silent, and yet that must be appealed to because it *is* God. It is ultimately God who is cannibalistically gorging on the bodies of babies in Lamentations, as the poem makes clear in its images of mouth and hand. "The Lord hath swallowed up all the habitations of Jacob, and hath not pitied . . . he hath bent his bow like an enemy . . . he hath not withdrawn his hand from destroying" (2.2, 4, 8). The horrifying sublime prepares for, explains, and contains the horrifying pathetic: "The hands of the pitiful women have sodden [i.e. boiled] their own children; they were their meat in the destruction of the daughter of my people. The Lord hath accomplished his fury" (4.10–11). Ginsberg's generation has likewise been swallowed up by a more than human force, as the figurative conclusion of "Howl" I—the butchered heart of the poem of life "good to eat a thousand years" is literalized in the opening line of Part II: it is likewise a God who "bashed open their skulls and ate up their brains and imagination."

A pause here for Ginsberg's "Moloch," that sublimely elaborate invention of part II:

> Moloch! Solitude! Filth! Ugliness! Ashcans and unobtainable
> dollars! Children screaming under the stairways! Boys
> sobbing in armies! Old men weeping in the parks!
> Moloch! Moloch! Nightmare of Moloch! Moloch the loveless!
> Mental Moloch! Moloch the heavy judger of men!
> Moloch the incomprehensible prison! Moloch the crossbone
> soulless jailhouse and Congress of sorrows! Moloch
> whose buildings are judgment; Moloch the vast stone
> of war! Moloch the stunned governments! . . .

The name is derived from the Canaanite God of fire, Molech, to whom children were offered in sacrifice and whose worship by the Israelites is condemned in Leviticus, 1 and 2 Kings, Jeremiah, Amos, and Ezekiel: "Moreover thou hast taken thy sons and daughters whom thou hast borne unto me, and these thou hast sacrificed unto them to be devoured. Is this of thy whoredoms a small matter, that thou hast slain my children and delivered them to cause them to pass through the fire for them?" (Ezekiel 16.20–21). Israelite society for several centuries intermittently practiced human sacrifice which in theory it rejected. America, "Howl" Part II tells us, does the same. William Blake's Moloch represents the obsessive human sacrifice of war, especially as connected with perversely suppressed sexuality. Ginsberg's mind-forged Moloch likewise has this aspect, and is a broadly Urizenic figure for the oppressiveness of a modern industrial and military state, exuded from Reason. Ginsberg's Moloch is also the modern version of Mammon, the capitalism of "Unobtainable dollars . . . running money . . . electricity and banks!" But although you cannot worship both God and Mammon, Moloch is not an alternative to God, Moloch *is* God: "heavy judger of men . . . endless Jehovahs . . . They broke their backs lifting Moloch to Heaven!" Inorganic, abstract, Moloch is simultaneously within us and without us, incubus and whale's belly: "Moloch who entered my soul early! Moloch in whom I am a consciousness without a body!" Inescapable Moloch parallels the God of Lamentations.

The contradiction of a God who is also an enemy leads to a deeper contradiction central to the genre of lamentation and, it has been argued, to Jewishness itself. Chapter 3 of Lamentations, its longest chapter, centers on a fusion of despair and hope: "He hath turned aside my ways, and pulled me in pieces" turns itself inside out with "The Lord is my portion, saith my soul; therefore have I hope" (3.11, 21). "Out of the mouth of the Most High proceedeth not evil and good?" (3.38). As literature and as consolation, the poem of lamentation "must communicate its own inadequacy. Its success, in a sense, depends on its failure."[9] When Ginsberg's manic "Footnote to Howl" announces the holiness of everything, it produces an absurd, irrational, extravagant inversion of Part I. Like the hope of the author of Lamentations, Ginsberg's celebration is not logical but willed:

> Holy! Holy! Holy! Holy! Holy! Holy! Holy! Holy! Holy!
>> Holy! Holy! Holy! Holy! Holy! Holy!
> The world is holy! The soul is holy! The skin is holy!
>> The nose is holy! The tongue and cock and hand
>> and asshole holy!
> Everything is holy! everybody's holy! everywhere is
>> holy! everyday is in eternity! Everyman's an
>> angel!

This ecstatic revelation has its literary source in the "Holy, holy, holy" shout of the seraphim praising God in Isaiah 6.3, but as in Blake's "Marriage of Heaven and Hell," which is clearly one of Ginsberg's most important models here, "everything that lives is holy." Whitman, too, had claimed "Divine am I inside and out, and I make holy whatever I touch or am touched from: The scent of these arm-pits is aroma finer than prayer." Further, as "Holy" inverts "howly," what has previously been interpreted as monstrous by the poet himself may now be reinterpreted:

> Holy the solitudes of skyscrapers and pavements! Holy
>> the cafeterias filled with the millions! Holy the
>> mysterious rivers of tears under the streets!

in a spurt of hilarity, even Moloch can and must be included:

> Holy time in eternity holy eternity in time holy the
>> clocks in space holy the fourth dimension holy
>> the fifth International holy the Angel in Moloch!

And finally

> Holy the supernatural extra brilliant intelligent
>> kindness of the soul!

Kindness again. That almost imperceptible Yiddish kindness. It is perhaps of interest that Ginsberg apparently thought the poem finished after Part III, and mailed copies to numerous friends and critics, including Richard Eberhart, to whom he wrote an extended formal discussion of the poem without the footnote on May 18, 1956, and including his father. He received a letter from Louis dated February 29, 1956: "I am gratified about your new ms. It's a wild, rhapsodic, explosive outpouring with good figures of speech flashing by in its volcanic rushing. . . . It's a hot geyser of emotion suddenly released in wild abandon from subterranean depths of your being." Louis insisted, however, "there is no need for dirty, ugly words, as they will entangle you unnecessarily in trouble," and added his anxiety that the poem "is a one-sided neurotic view of life, it has not enough glad, Whitmanic affirmations."[10] Sweet, embarrassed, embarrassing Louis. And did Allen perhaps compose the footnote under the invisible pressure of his father's admonition?

III. It Occurs to Him That He Is America

> To be a Jew in the twentieth century
> Is to be offered a gift. If you refuse,
> Wishing to be invisible, you choose
> Death of the spirit, the stone insanity.
> Accepting, take full life. Full agonies:
> Your evening deep in labyrinthine blood
> Of those who resist, fail and resist; and God
> Reduced to a hostage among hostages.
>
> The gift is torment. Not alone the still
> Torture, isolation; or torture of the flesh.
> That may come also. But the accepting wish,
> The whole and fertile spirit as guarantee
> For every human freedom, suffering to be free,
> Daring to live for the impossible.

That is of course Rukeyser again, the Rukeyser of "Letter to the Front," published in 1944, stylistically a world away from "Howl," chronologically a decade away, morally shoulder to queer Jewish shoulder. How Jewish then is the Ginsberg of "Howl"? I have been attempting to suggest both a low Yiddish element and a high Hebraic element in that poem, notwithstanding what must also be spoken of: the poet as a "Jew in flight from Judaism," or what Isaac Deutscher called "the non-Jewish Jew."

His ethnicity was never exactly invisible to others. "Naive, he was incredibly naive," recalled Lucien Carr of his fellow student at Columbia. "He was just an eager young Jewish kid from Paterson who wanted to know everything about books and writers and art and painting." Kerouac fictionalizes the young Allen in *The Town and the City* (1946): "Levinsky was an eager, sharply intelligent boy of Russian-Jewish parentage who rushed around New York in a perpetual sweat of emotional activity." And in *The Vanity of Duluoz:* "I was sitting in Edie's apartment one day when the door opened and in walks this spindly Jewish kid with horn-rim glasses and tremendous ears sticking out, 17 years old, burning black eyes, a strangely deep voice."[11] Introducing *Empty Mirror,* William Carlos Williams calls Ginsberg "this young Jewish boy," before going on to compare him with Dante and Chaucer, but then comes around to paralleling him with "the prophet Jeremiah." Richard Eberhart, describing Ginsberg's performance of "Howl" at the Six Gallery reading for the September 2, 1956, *New York Times Book Review,* writes: "My first reaction was that it is based on destructive violence. It is profoundly Jewish in temper. It is Biblical in its repetitive grammatical buildup. It is a howl against anything in our mechanistic civilization which kills the spirit." M. L. Rosenthal, reviewing "Howl" in the *Nation* in 1957, wrote that the poem had "the single-minded frenzy of a raving madwoman" (brilliant guesswork, one might say; Naomi *is* that madwoman, for it can be argued that "Howl" ventriloquizes her voice just as the speaker of Lamentations ventriloquizes Jerusalem's, although "Kaddish" has not been published yet) but that some of Ginsberg's early poems at the back of the book "have a heavy Yiddish melancholy."[12] (Rosenthal in conversation with me called the "madwoman" a "typo," which he feared was insulting to both women and homosexuals and later changed to *madman,* but I would say he guessed better than he knew.) Edward Albee remembers Allen in the late fifties as "you young, a young old testament prophet." For Hayden Carruth he is "mindpetal, spectre, strangest jew, cityboy." Yevgeny Yevtushenko, who with a charm equal to

Allen's own calls him the "Omm-issar of American Poetry," remembers the beats as "the uprising of the garbage dumps of the suburbs. . . . And riding bareback on a garbage can, careering wildly past the Plaza and the Hilton, like a Jewish Mowgli of the concrete jungles, came Allen Ginsberg, prophet of the outpouring."[13]

෨

As to Allen's own testimony, "At 14 I was an introvert, an atheist, a Communist and a Jew, and I still wanted to be president of the United States."[14] His family listened to Eddie Cantor on the radio, and "it was a . . . high point of the week. I guess because he was Jewish and a national comedian and everybody in the family identified with him."[15] In the last year of high school Ginsberg vowed to devote his life to helping the working classes if he got into Columbia University. The simplicity of these identifications and that identity failed to outlast his crossing the river to Columbia and his immediate attraction to the bohemian likes of Lucien Carr, Jack Kerouac, William Burroughs, Neil Cassady, all non-Jews, apolitical, amoral. What was a nice Jewish boy doing with these types? Poor Louis kept asking. What did he have in mind by writing "Fuck the Jews" accompanied by a skull and crossbones on his dusty dorm window? Ginsberg's biographer Barry Miles takes Allen's word at face value that his little naughtiness was to catch the attention of an Irish cleaningwoman he suspected of being anti-Semitic. "Trilling and his wife were utterly unable to accept that Allen was simply goading the anti-Semitic Irish cleaner and years later Diana Trilling was still using the incident as an example of Ginsberg's 'Jewish self-hatred'."[16]

A few chapters later Barry Miles observes that Ginsberg "was unable to relate to his Jewish heritage."[17] How very Jewish. Carl Solomon, the dedicatee of "Howl," publishes his "Report from the Asylum: Afterthoughts of a Shock patient" under the name Carl Goy. Allen's brother Eugene changes his surname to Brooks when he becomes a lawyer. It would be years before Allen started identifying himself humorously as a Jewish Buddhist. When Ginsberg cites the sources and precedents for "Howl," he includes Blake, Shelley, Whitman, Christopher

Smart, Charlie Parker, Cézanne, Wilhelm Reich, Leadbelly, William Carlos Williams, Rimbaud, Céline, Brecht, Jean Genet, Hart Crane, and Tristan Corbière, to name a few. He names no Jewish source, and commenting on the phrase "bop kabbalah" distances himself from it as a bit of "mystical name-dropping" and says he had read "little on kabbalah."[18]

&

Two interesting essays by fellow poets touch on this matter of Ginsberg's reluctance to identify with Jewishness—his wish to "pass" as an unmarked member of the Euro-American avant-garde—through meditating on the ancient heavenly connection of Allen-Naomi. To Clayton Eshleman, Ginsberg's "visionary panic over the destructiveness of North American society, the way it titillates the self and then cold-cocks it," derives from how "on a very personal level, North America had done the same thing to his mother . . . it is the agony of the son who escorted his mother when he was twelve to the asylum . . . that flows through the magnificent first movement of 'Howl.' . . . Ginsberg would save Mankind since he was unable to save Naomi."[19] This seems to me entirely correct. Supporting Eshleman's intuition we might notice that the nominal "secret hero" of Part I may be Neil Cassady, "N.C. . . . cocksman and Adonis of Denver," but toward the close of Part I comes a set of lines whose reference is Carl Solomon, and in its midst "the mother finally ******" and the yellow paper rose twisted on a wire hanger in the nameless Naomi's madhouse closet. In a letter to John Hollander Ginsberg calls the "Footnote" "too serious a joke to explain" and then explains it by saying its real dedicatee is "my mother who died in the madhouse and it says I loved her anyway."[20] Having said this, the letter then hastens to return to technical talk about "open prophetic bardic poetry." Allen Grossman, in a partially skewed essay on Ginsberg, "The Jew as American Poet," argues that "the Jew, like the Irishman, presents himself as the type of the sufferer in history" but that for Ginsberg the beat subculture "takes the place of the real ethnic and political subcultures which in the past succored and gave identity to the outcast by forming a community of outcasts." "In 'Kaddish,' " Grossman continues, "the archetypal female is a mutilated and paranoid old woman ('scars of operations, pancreas, belly wounds, abortions, appendix, stitching of incisions pulling down in the fat like hideous thick zippers') haunted by the image of Hitler and dying, obscene and abandoned, in the sanitarium. This is Ginsberg's version of the Jewish mother and, simultaneously, of the shechina, the wandering soul of Israel herself." Surely this is correct, and surely what is expressed in "Kaddish" is repressed but powerfully latent in "Howl"—so much so that one may almost feel the son's voice to be that of the mother. Does he speak for her, or is she speaking through him? This is as impossible to decide as it is to identify the voice of Lamentations as witness *or* victim. And if Naomi is the invisible mother/matter of Ginsberg's first great poem, there is an uncanny connection between this mother who almost devoured her son and the mothers who cannibalize their infants in the streets of Jerusalem. Grossman goes on, however, to claim that Ginsberg "erects on [Naomi's] grave an image which is no longer ethnic and which therefore is no longer obsessed by the mystery of the Jewish people in history" and to remark that "throughout Ginsberg's writing there is an ambivalence toward Jewishness which should be recognized as it seems to be an emphatic part of his public statement."[21] Grossman is implying, I think, that Ginsberg is somehow or other not a *real* Jew because of this.

Yet ambivalence toward Jewishness, like pepper in the stew, is a key ingredient of post-Enlightenment Jewish writing. Alan Mintz, tracing "responses to catastrophe in Hebrew literature" from Lamentations to the post-Holocaust era, stresses four historic stances: First, there is an early rabbinic theme of *shame* at Israel's humiliation before the nations, quite apart from the insistence on Israel's sinfulness. During the late medieval period, in response to arbitrary Christian massacres of Jews, there develops an exaltation of suffering as "an opportunity awarded by God to the most worthy for the display of righteousness." In the early modern period, from the 1880s to the early 1900s, writers like Shalom Abromowitsch, Saul Tchernichevsky, and Chaim Nachman Bialik respond to the devastating pogroms that swept Russia and Eastern Europe with a literature of profound and bitter ambivalence toward the masses of Jewish

people—part pity, part contempt. And in the Palmach genera-
tion of Israeli writers the dominant stance toward the Euro-
pean victims of the holocaust was indeed contempt.

To be a Jew in diaspora is to be ambivalent. It is commonly
also to take on the colors of the host culture. To be more
German than the Germans, like Heine; more French than the
French, like Dreyfuss, Sartre, and Simone Weil; more English
than the English, like Disraeli; more Russian than the Rus-
sians, like Isaac Babel, who rode with the cossacks. Would
someone named Bobby Zimmerman have had the extraordi-
nary effect on American youth wielded by someone named
Bob Dylan? To believe in the host culture's own ideals about
itself and then to write as an indignant social critic when the
host nation fails (of course) to embody those ideals: this is all
normal for the Jewish writer.

Yet Allen as Jew remains a good son. From his father's
socialism, that tenderhearted materialism. Allen keeps and
intensifies the tenderness while questioning the materialism.
Of his mother's communism—her paranoid idealism—Allen
tries to exorcise the paranoia (everything's holy, Moloch is
holy, breathe deep and say Om) while holding fast to the
idealism, free love and all, physical and emotional nudism and
all. From Louis's poetry he retains a devotion to form. From
Naomi's madness he retains the outrageousness and outgrows
the self-destructiveness.

From America Allen takes Whitman. The manly love of
comrades, the open road, the democratic vistas stretching to
eternity, and also the eyes of America taking a fall, which he
plants, later, in his mother's head. America will always be, for
him, infinite hope and infinite disappointment. That's very
Jewish.

And from Judaism he takes the universal compassion and
rejects the tribalism. Instead of professing victimization as Jew,
his writing projects victimization onto the world and in the
same moment proposes, through the mystery of rhetoric, to
save it. The power of prophetic rhetoric in the genre of Lam-
entation is that it must wring cosmic affirmation out of de-
spair. God is your enemy, and you must trust him. Moloch
whose eyes are a thousand blind windows eats his children,

but you must declare him holy. A decade after completing "Howl," Ginsberg at the climax of "Wichita Vortex Sutra" calls "all the powers of the Imagination" to his side and declares "the end of the War." Ridiculous, absurd, foolish, impossible. Daring to live for the impossible.

NOTES

My thanks to Maeera Shreiber for instigating this essay, and for valuable suggestions.

1. Ted Enslin is succinct and typical: "Many years ago I wrote a collection of short takes on various poets, attempting to capture an outstanding characteristic of each one. When it came to Allen it was simply 'KINDNESS,' and I let it stand as that single word. One does not enhance such a quality by modifiers or explanation" (see *Best Minds: A Tribute to Allen Ginsberg*, ed. Bill Morgan and Bob Rosenthal [New York: Lospeccio Press, 1986], 100). Tuli Kupferberg, ex-Fug, accompanies a ditty to "Al the Gins / A Jewish Prins" with a cartoon of self and Ginsberg, the balloon of the first saying, "Hey Allen what's the good word" and the second answering "Kindness" (*Best Minds*, 159). Jane Kramer's *Allen Ginsberg in America* (New York: Random House, 1969) represents Ginsberg as unfailingly generous, compassionate, and saintly. On the other hand, Bruce Cook in *The Beat Generation* (New York: Scribner's, 1981) argues that the young Allen was "an aggressive, savage young man . . . a great hater," whose anguish was healed only by the satori experienced after his exhausting and fruitless stay in India, on the Kyoto-Tokyo Express. And at least two commentators on "Howl" seem, interestingly, offended by the poem's swerve from the "anger" they feel ought to be its core. Michael Rumaker in *Black Mountain Review* (fall 1957) claims that "the impact of the anger" was corrupted "by sentimentality, bathos, Buddha." Clayton Eshleman appears to agree, complaining that "Howl III" "is very close to being cute" instead of pursuing "the direction toward an unqualified attack on the sensibility-destroying aspect of North America" (*Idaho Review*, 109).

2. Irving Howe and Eliezer Greenberg, eds., *A Treasury of Yiddish Stories* (New York: Viking, 1954), 37–38.

3. A notable example is Rexroth's defense of "Howl" in his trial statement: "The simplest term for such writing is prophetic, it is easier to call it that than anything else because we have a large body of prophetic writing to refer to. There are the prophets in the Bible

which it greatly resembles in purpose and in language and in subject matter . . . the theme is the denunciation of evil and a pointing of the way out, so to speak. That is prophetic literature." In Lewis Hyde, ed. *On the Poetry of Allen Ginsberg* (Ann Arbor: University of Michigan Press, 1984), 50.

4. Jan Wojcik and Raymond-Jean Frontain, *Poetic Prophecy in Western Literature* (Cranbury, N.J.: Associated University Presses, 1984), 9–10. Herbert N. Schneider, *Sacred Discontent: the Bible in Western Tradition* (Berkeley: University of California Press, 1976).

5. See Barry Miles, *Ginsberg: A Biography* (New York: Viking, 1989), 187–89.

6. I will not dwell here on the differences, which of course are also major—among them the fact that Ginsberg seems to have no conception of sin; that "Howl" is not literally theistic (Moloch and Jehovah are for Ginsberg mind-forged gods as they were for Blake); and that parts 1 and 3 are very funny as well as sensationally plangent.

7. Alan Mintz, *Ḥurban: Responses to Catastrophe in Hebrew Literature* (New York: Columbia University Press, 1984), 3–4.

8. Ibid., x.

9. Francis Landy, "Lamentations," in Robert Alter and Frank Kermode, eds., *The Literary Guide to the Bible* (Cambridge: Harvard University Press), 329–30. Landy argues (333) that "the enactment of inadequacy" and hopelessness in Lamentations is ultimately mitigated in the absence of a divine reply by the beauty and formality of the poetry—the acrostics whose "assurance and freedom counteract the loss of political and religious structure described in the poem."

10. Miles, *Ginsberg*, 204.

11. Ibid., 42, 74, 44.

12. Hyde, 17–18, 25, 29, 31.

13. *Best Minds*, 5, 53.

14. Allen Ginsberg, *Journals: Early Fifties, Early Sixties*, ed. Gordon Ball (New York: Grove Press, 1977), 17.

15. Miles, *Ginsberg*, 19.

16. Ibid., 59–61.

17. Ibid., 210.

18. Allen Ginsberg, *Howl: Original Draft Facsimile, Transcript and Variant Versions . . . Fully Annotated by Author*, ed. Barry Miles (New York: HarperCollins, 1995), 126.

19. Hyde, *On the Poetry of Allen Ginsberg*, 109, 112.

20. Ginsberg, *Howl*, 163.

21. Hyde, *On the Poetry of Allen Ginsberg*, 102, 103, 105, 199.

Afterword

The essays in this book may or may not be pearls. But most of them formed around some grain of intellectual or emotional irritation. The title essay responds to critics for whom "politics" and "poetry" must be forever separate categories—and still more to those who suppose that the women's poetry movement of the post-1960s period has nothing to contribute in formal and aesthetic terms to poetry. The position is a familiar but ignorant one. The essay on Whitman was initially intended as pure homage to Walt's multilayered eroticism; in the middle of its composition the United States commenced bombing Iraq, and I was forced uncomfortably to recognize not only that Whitman's enthusiastic support of the War between the States was a predictable outcome of that eroticism, but that War and Love were, for him, indissolubly linked.

The unlikely-seeming combination of Elisabeth Bishop and Sharon Olds as objects of a critical essay was not my own idea. Disturbed by another critic who seemed unable to praise one without demeaning the other, I was stimulated to track their likenesses. They are, I discovered with fascination, like shadow images of each other in the representation of eros; in one, when we read between the lines of fear we find desire, while in the other the reverse is the case. The investigation also confirmed for me how risky it is to write with, or about, love, in a literary climate wedded to coolness and impersonality. A version of the essay given at a conference confirmed something else, however: there exists a secret thirst for love poetry among academics as well as among ordinary folk. I would be happy to encourage this thirst.

To write about Maxine Kumin was a long-standing intention of mine, as Maxine has been for me a model of sanity and reasonableness combined with attachment to life and to the natural world. What precipitated this essay, however, was a sudden hunch that Kumin's nature poetry was not merely sane. It was revolutionary in the history of nature writing— merely by virtue of refusing to imagine that anything (including our selves) could possibly be *superior* to nature. Writing of Lucille Clifton, whom I have adored for years, posed several kinds of challenges. How could I demonstrate that Clifton belongs in the mainstream of poetry in our language, not in a ghetto? How could I follow her into a realm of religious experience that seemed to grow more mysterious with each new volume? And how could I deal with the inevitable and pained sense of exclusion I found myself at times feeling as a white woman reading Clifton's work?

The closing essay, on Allen Ginsberg, comes directly from my own midlife explorations of Judaism. It pleased Allen to keep his cultural distance from Judaism, but did he fool anyone? Is there an American poet more rabbinical? "Kaddish" is of course an obviously Jewish poem, but the task I set myself was to dig for the Jewishness latent in the earlier breakthrough work, "Howl." Having begun with the hypothesis that "Howl" might share some of its poetic characteristics with the biblical Book of Lamentations—a work in a comparable genre—I ended by discovering a more complicatedly Jewish Ginsberg than I had suspected.

From each of the poets discussed in this book I have learned something immeasurable. The essays are by way of thanks.